LAWRENCE VIGGIANO

Two. Three.

Who is the G.O.A.T.?

D1516703

I dedicate this book to Kobe Bryant, a man taken far too soon with his most profound contributions still ahead of him, a man who was everything we should aspire to be as competitors and winners. He is often overlooked in the G.O.A.T. debate for reasons unknown to me. Perhaps, after some time, there will be a sequel... . Kobe, thank you for the memories; this one is for you.

Contents

Acknowledgement

Writing this book has been so much more rewarding than I could have ever imagined. None of this would have been possible without my family and friends; thank you for being my biggest fans and harshest critics. Your love pushes me to be the best I can be and your honesty grounds me. I would like to explicitly thank my parents for sacrificing to give me more opportunity than I could ever ask for, the motivation to succeed and tough love I often need. I also want to thank everyone who transformed my love for the game of basketball into my peace and passion, my place to escape and unwind, one 21-point game at a time.

I

Introduction

The jerseys are out there. We know who wears the Two. Three. But, who is number one?

1

What is a G.O.A.T.?

G.O.A.T. Translation: Greatest of All Time. We universally agree with the acronym, but that's about it. We typically reserve this designation for athletes, musicians, movie stars, etc. As the old expression goes, *"Opinions are like assholes, everyone has one and most of them stink."* The year is 2020, so before I get cancelled in the opening paragraph, if there is a demographic that is offended by the expression, stop reading now and find a safe space; this is not for you.

We can all agree on what G.O.A.T means, but who is the G.O.A.T: Ali? Tyson? Mayweather? Brady? Jay-Z? Nas? Drake? Tiger? Serena? Federer? MJ? Kobe? LeBron? Messi? Ronaldo? I know, I know – I left someone off or put someone on you don't agree with, but that's exactly the point.

Everyone has their own bias and opinion and it often becomes a geographical or generational argument based on personal preference, not backed by facts. Imagine if we could remove opinion and come to an answer based solely in FACT. Nothing wrong with saying that you prefer Messi to Ronaldo or vice versa, but there is probably a clear-cut answer, whether you have the pride to admit it is a different question. The latter is why sports have been and will continue to be so impactful around the globe.

How many times have we seen brawls break out at sporting events because another human being walked past with a different color jersey? To someone who does not care for sports and competition, such a situation would warrant a facepalm or eye-roll emoji, but to the rest of us (the normal ones), we immediately want to know who won and say things like, *"Philly fans are trash"* or *"But, the Yankees are the classiest franchise, right?"*. Not to get on Philly, but were there not viral videos of Eagles' fans actually eating horseshit after they won Super Bowl LII?

How about Bills Mafia? I know Buffalo is cold and you have to make life interesting but jumping off of a school bus in below twenty-degree temps through a folding table... PRE-GAME! C'mon Philly and Buffalo, do better!

But no, if you are a true diehard fan, there's a part of you that shrugs your shoulders a bit and shakes your head back and forth, giving the Larry David, "Eh, okay, okay." We all cannot be Cologero from *A Bronx Tale* and throw away the Mickey Mantle card because, as Sonny put it, "Mickey Mantle don't care about you, so why should you care about him?"[1]

Rivalry, hatred for and comradery between and amongst fans

of teams and organizations conjure this unparalleled and indescribable pride. Picture the World Cup; the starting elevens scream their respective national anthems, sometimes in tears, because of the passion they have for their jersey, flag and country (except America, we kneel and protest wages…another topic for another day). So why have I gone off on a tangent this early on? The essence of sports – pride and rivalry – triggers great debates.

Without further ado, which *two-three* is *the G.O.A.T.?*

2

Comparisons

As you may have noticed from the cover, our great debate in this text will be, *"Who is the G.O.A.T., King James or Air Jordan?"*

But, why? Why must we compare and argue? Why can't we just appreciate true greatness as it unfolds before our eyes? Before I offer the simple answer, this question brings to mind the satirical *This is SportsCenter* commercial with Rich Eisen and the late-great, Stuart Scott, observing Kobe go to a vending machine for some potato chips. Eisen and Scott spent a few seconds saying, *"very Jordan-esque"* and *"that's exactly what Jordan would have picked."* [2]

It's what we do as humans. We compare. We have been conditioned to judge and compare in all facets of life. The media does it to stir up controversy and rack up viewership. It is inherently wrong and, at the end of the day, we can probably all agree that instead of comparing Kobe to Jordan for *x* number of years, we should have just marveled at their individual successes and greatness, but we'll continue to do it over and over again, just substituting the names.

It begs the question, *His Airness* or *The Chosen One*? Let's dive into the FACTS and not your crazy uncle's, nor your nutcase P.S.A.L. coach's, nor the playground court old head's biased arguments, or even, dare I say it, your barber's. I apologize in advance for the deafening silence that will flood barbershops worldwide. Tell them to throw a copy of this book on top of all the old magazines that nobody opens anyway and spend more time cutting hair. Let's end this debate once and for all.

Before we get scientific, let's answer the question I am hoping you would all be smart enough to ask: *Who is this arrogant prick that thinks he can end a debate that will assuredly carry on for decades after this is published?*

II

About Your Author

3

Queens Forever

I am new to the whole writing thing, but not too new to know that this section is typically dedicated to the back cover with a professional headshot in a turtleneck in front of a wood-burning fire. Trust me, I am not taking this unconventional approach out of vanity. I want to paint a picture so you understand my inherent bias and what I value about this game so that you can strip me of it when analyzing MJ and LBJ.

First and most important note – sorry, Tim Riggins, but it's actually *Queens Forever*. Shout out to Ron Artest, Lamar Odom, Anthony Mason, Kenny Smith, Kenny Anderson, Raefer Alston, a.k.a. Skip to My Lou, Stephen A. Smith and so many other influential coaches, players and basketball minds that have claimed parts of Queens over the years.

For those of you who don't know what NYC basketball is like, I am so terribly sorry. If you never waited hours only to get left on zip at the West 4th Street Courts or watched a summer league pro-am at Dyckman or the Rucker or heard the legend of Sweetwater Clifton, Dr. J or Lew Alcindor before he was Kareem, again, I am so terribly sorry.

If you know any of the players that I have mentioned, you know they all have one thing in common – *that New York toughness*. If you're not from here, you wouldn't understand, unless of course, you have had the pleasure of playing a pickup game against a few New Yorkers.

My uncle was recently telling me a story that is perfect to illustrate this toughness. He was playing at Laguna Beach in California, where I have also had some good runs. To keep it short, he and some buddies got on the court and remained there all day because naturally, *Queens get the money*. As they were coming off the court, one of the opponents asked if they were from New York, to which the group immediately thought that they were taking jabs at their accents or slang. Nope, try again. He said that it was the way they beat the shit out of him on defense. Believe the story or not, just go watch a Ron Artest or Anthony Mason highlight video. You might understand. The point is that New York basketball is recognized across the country and around the world.

When I say the world, I mean it. See God Shammgod and Russ Smith. God Shammgod has a move named after him that is used on every continent where basketball is played. Russ Smith, for those of you that don't know, scored 65, the most points ever in a single game in the NBA Development League, now known as the NBA G League.[3] Even more impressive, this NYC legend averaged a 60-piece in China's NBL and that's no exaggeration. As a matter of fact, I did him an injustice; he averaged 61.2![4] Ever heard of *Starbury*? The man has statues and a museum over 6,800 miles from Coney Island in Beijing!

Now, I am nowhere near the player those guys are, but if you go to my park and mention my name, there will for sure be *G.O.A.T.* comments (we can debate that in the sequel). Not meant to toot my own horn, but more so to show what I value – killer mentality; hard-nosed, non-stop pressure on defense; some flash and cockiness; grit and no quit. Those would be my intangibles for the *G.O.A.T.* archetype in *2K*.

I want to give a quick tribute to my father because without him assuming the role of Bill Laimbeer and Rick Mahorn in the driveway games from when I was six years old on an eight-foot hoop, I wouldn't have understood what makes this game great.

4

June 5, 1999

Intertwined with my New York-style understanding of the game is my love of the game. I had already been playing instructional basketball and attending camps in the summer for a year or so, but my love of the game was confirmed on June 5, 1999, my first time at *The Garden*, and not that bullshit arena they call *The Garden* in Boston – I am talking about *The World's Most Famous Arena*.

I didn't follow the league too tightly back then; I was just over six years old, but I went through the box scores at the back of the *NY Daily News* every day. I knew that we just beat Miami – thank you Alan Houston – and swept Atlanta rather lightly. I also knew that Big Pat was out with an injury. And above all, I knew Reggie Miller was not as good as his sister Cheryl, as well as some other words I was told not to repeat when my uncle yelled at the television because the Knicks didn't cover the spread. We were three wins (against our nemesis) Pacers away from the NBA Finals, so I was hyped to go to my first live-action, pro game.

14

For those of you that don't know about *The Garden* and probably a lot of venues back in the day, if you knew people, you could sneak in without a ticket, go all the way down to the floor-level seats, and with a crisp twenty-dollar bill to the right usher, boom, that's your seat for the game – even if the hedge fund, season ticket holder showed up with his mistress after halftime. You gotta love New York!

Something unique to the Garden was the code to get past the turnstiles without a ticket for that game – pretty sure my uncle gave my dad a Barbara Streisand concert ticket stub from 1996 to get us through. In the car, we rehearsed, "Junior, what do we say at the gate when they take the ticket?"

"*Billy A.*" If you know, you know. And sure as shit, it worked. I can still remember walking down to the court, jaw probably dragging the ground. Lights, music, and as always, a rowdy crowd of Knicks fans getting ready for what we didn't know at the time was about to be one of the most historic moments in Garden history.

I was overwhelmed as you could imagine. Clapping and screaming at every basket, checking the scoreboard each time to make sure they were adding it up correctly.

Fast forward to the good part. These sons of bitches were up 91-88 with under 12 seconds to go and we had the rock.

So much went wrong here that I found out later in life, but at the time, all I knew was that LJ gave Antonio Davis some serious face time. And one. One official signaled the three and the other called the foul. The Garden didn't stop rocking until LJ stepped to the line to stick his free throw. Everyone remained standing, but a brief hush broke up the roars for a moment as Mark Jackson put up a teardrop that never had a chance. Triple-zeroes. 92-91. Ball game. Unbelievable. The rocking at the Garden resumed and there was a semi-court storming. Ruckus spilled onto 33rd Street. I couldn't sleep that night.

I would be remiss to not tell the parts of this story that should have ruined my first game so that the Knicks wouldn't have earned the opportunity to break my heart as they have over the next twenty-plus years.

First off, Reggie Miller should have had a shot to deliver one of his many *Garden* daggers, and Larry Bird didn't draw something up on the play before the *Four-Point Play*, nor the possession following.

Next, former Heisman Trophy winner, Charlie Ward, was inbounding over the much taller and longer lanky-ass, Jalen Rose. I guess the offensive line at FSU wasn't too tall because a QB1 should be able to get the ball over. But, of course, Rose got a mitt on it, giving Knicks fans ulcers and starting the clock a little earlier than it should have, blowing up the play that Van Gundy was running for Houston, the hero against the Heat in Game 7 of the first round.

This caused LJ to catch it and give an impromptu performance of a few jab steps, a pump, one dribble, pull-up over Antonio Davis. A few things from that sequence:

How in the hell do you not foul as he's dancing damn-near 30 feet from the basket? How do you, then, foul on the SHOT!?

Would LJ have had the game he had if not for the odd circumstances of the strike-shortened and rushed season that caused Pat to get hurt? Would he have even been on the floor if Pat was healthy?

The perfect storm. And that was *my* moment. Naturally, the guy with the same name as me, Larry Johnson (I'm Larry Jr. a.k.a., "LJ"), sinks a game-winner on my first game at the Garden and sure enough, is running down the court throwing his patented fist-to-elbow, makeshift "L" up when the clock hit triple-zero. From that moment on, I loved the game. I, unfortunately, developed an undying love for *those* Knicks and the way they played the game.

Okay, enough being sentimental. Why is this necessary to frame the argument about LeBron and Mike? Directly, there's not much of a reason other than if Jordan doesn't leave the game for the second time before the start of this season, are the Knicks afforded this opportunity? But, indirectly, many of my basketball values and what I consider greatness come from that game: NYC grit, jail ball defense, next man up mentality, underdog Cinderella team, hard work over talent, etc.

5

My Generation & My Preference

W hile I am a Knicks fan to the core, I am and always will be a student of the game and a fan of pure team basketball. Some of the other teams I have enjoyed watching and respected over the years have been Pop's dynastic Spurs, which is ironic considering they ruined the Knicks' 1999 Cinderella story, the 2004 Pistons, Riley's 2006 Heat, the 2011 Mavs, among others who didn't get to raise the trophy like Thibodeau's Bulls, the current Jazz and C's led by Quin Snyder and Brad Stephens, respectively.

These teams defied convention in one way or another, implemented a well-led, culture-driven, team game with defensive emphasis and ego absent.

I wish I could watch hypothetical games up against the current, dare I say, *Curry-era* style teams on a loop. I truly believe it has ruined the game, but ultimately, the future has other plans for this style of play in my opinion. I also see the 2000s as the right mix of talent and skill, athleticism, remnants of nineties toughness, defense and system-driven basketball.

I have no interest in watching James Harden dribble for 17 seconds of a shot clock and hoist up a fade away from 23-feet, kick his legs out and shoot three free throws. I have no interest in watching Brook Lopez spot up for five contested three's in a single game, mostly with plenty of time on the shot clock at a 30-percent clip. I am not a fan of Zach Lavine (dunk contest is a different story), DeAngelo Russell, Andrew Wiggins, etc. (you get the idea). Also, not a fan of some of the new generation that doesn't want to work and is satisfied with losing and playing nonchalantly with prima donna attitudes – yes, KAT, you. I don't like the fashion shows before the games. I don't like the non-stop complaining and burners – that one is for those guys out in *Barclays*.

Don't get me wrong. There are some real dogs out there that I love watching and I think there are many more of them coming. I just want it to be about basketball. I understand you are more than an athlete; but when you go to work, I don't care about your fashion, your political opinions, and your best friend hugs for the other teams – I want to see the *Mamba Mentality;* I want to see the Larry Bird and Gary Payton-level shit-talking; I want to see tempers flare.

That's just me and what I want to see. Maybe I have become the old head, but that's basketball. On the playground, game twenty-one, five bucks a head, we're putting everything on the line, we're cheating scores, we're fouling hard on point game, and most importantly, we're talking all the shit. So, when you're getting paid hundreds of millions throughout your career, keep that same energy. That's how we came up playing and that's how we should go down. That same hunger that got you to the league should never leave on that 94 by 55. I understand it's a business and you're about the bag, but you'll never be able to convince me otherwise about how basketball should be played. Period.

6

My Quick Take: James or Jordan?

Based on my previous rant, you already know which way I personally lean in the debate. Air Jordan over everybody. LeBron's not in my top-five either, Paul Pierce. In fairness, he might make it up there when it's all said and done. But, as of the end of the 2018-2019 season, I'm taking Larry Bird as my best small forward of all-time (side note, one of the most underrated players of all-time and I can admit that even though I have been taught to hate Boston from a very young age).

How can I say something like that? Would the media personalities roast me for it? I have one simple response in the form of a question...*why do you play?* In the words of the great Herm Edwards as the coach of the New York Jets, "This is what the greatest thing about sports is: You play to win the game! Hello?! You play to win the game!"[5]

At this point in time, I cannot call somebody the *G.O.A.T.* if he has come up short on the biggest stage six times and counting, not to mention the most embarrassing loss of them all as a BRONZE medalist in Athens in 2004.

Flip to the Jordan side of the coin. One word. Undefeated. Need I say more? Okay, fine, no Finals Game 7 necessary in six tries. Keep going? Okay, three-peat, quit in his prime, transformed his body and played pro baseball, 18-month hiatus and voila, three-peat AGAIN! Dream team alpha male. When you play to win the game and you're that dude on two dynasties or one super dynasty, however you would like to classify his stranglehold over 1990s basketball, I really don't see why there is any type of argument between these guys. If that's not enough, what about the shoes?

That's the short of it for me. However, these are opinions based on what I value and consider when talking about the *G.O.A.T.* We're going to lay it all out, get into the numbers, dig deeper into the numbers and go beyond the numbers. With all that being said, I can remove my *feelings* and spit *facts.* So, it's about that time to dive into it.

III

Kids

7

The Hype is Real

The social media age is something, isn't it? Broad statement, but let's focus the lens into perspective. *Real* basketball people will know names of high schools that certain pros who skipped college for the NBA attended: T-Mac; Mt. Zion Christian Academy; Amare, Cypress Creek; Dwight Howard, Southwest Atlanta Christian; KG, Farragut Academy; Kobe, Lower Merion[6] - okay enough showing off.

Some of us know them because we can recall David Stern saying them on draft night or from playing franchise mode in *NBA Live* or *2K*, or because it's a national powerhouse (e.g., Oak Hill), but did Drake *and* J. Cole put your high school on the map in a verse? They did for LeBron. Remember, this is before *Ballislife* and *ESPN*'s Bronny James segments.

Drake did during a freestyle for Tim Westwood *"I ain't lyin' to the kids, like the dentist ain't scary; I'm what LeBron was to St. Vincent-St. Mary's".*[7] J. Cole did on the *Down Bad* track, *"Now, little Jermaine got the same story as that boy out of St. Vincent, St.*

Mary: G.O.A.T".[8]

The Chosen One averaged 18 points per game as a freshman, scored 25 to secure a state title that year and followed it up by repeating as state champs and being named to the *USA Today All-USA First Team*, the first-ever sophomore to receive the honor. Year three, another state title and *Gatorade Player of the Year* and even contemplated going pro without finishing high school.[9]

Undoubtedly, he was destined for greatness, but what is even more impressive is the attention and coverage he drew to an otherwise unheard-of Ohio High School basketball program. This high school coverage was unlike anything before or to-date. LeBron was on *Sports Illustrated* covers and had daily *ESPN* segments before he was old enough to get a driver's license; that's next-level hype right there.

Following *ESPN*, came endorsements, signature shoes, etc. Big companies saw the marketing gift basket that was LeBron, similar to how they saw MJ about twenty years prior, and both benefitted tremendously from the *off-the-court* money.

However, in stark comparison, MJ didn't even make his varsity high school team until he was an upperclassman and you would be hard-pressed to find a casual fan that knows Jordan went to Laney HS. Clearly, he did well enough in his two years on varsity to be recruited by legendary coach, Dean Smith of the University of North Carolina at Chapel Hill, one of the most widely recognized collegiate powerhouses of all-time.

Even though the hype didn't come to MJ until college, it picked up fast. "Big Game" James Worthy, an NBA-legend in his own right and Tar Heel teammate of MJ, famously admitted in an interview with fellow Tar Heel-legend Antawn Jamison, *"I was better than MJ... for about three weeks."*[10]

Though his teammates and coaches knew of his talents and greatness, it took the country a bit longer. March Madness. Championship Monday. UNC, Georgetown. Down one with 18 seconds to go and this confident freshman pulls up from mid-range and sticks it. He went from Mike Jordan to MJ right there before America's eyes and never looked back.

LeBron and Jordan were both top-three picks, in arguably two of the best draft classes of all-time, with LeBron being number one overall in 2003 and Jordan being drafted third overall in 1984. I do believe a re-draft is in order for the first three picks, so let's pour one out for Houston, not that The Dream was a slouch by any means, and poor Portland because Sam Bowie should probably be pictured in *Merriam Webster* next to the words *bust* and *gaffe*. Don't worry, they redeemed themselves with Kevin Durant...ouch. Either way, not only was there a ton of hype, expectations were sky-high for two players going to franchises in peril.

8

Great or G.O.A.T?

The hype was real, no question; these guys were both destined for greatness and potentially, *G.O.A.T.* status. So, what makes you the *G.O.A.T.?* We established what my *G.O.A.T.* archetype intangibles are, but what can we all agree enshrines a *great as* the *G.O.A.T.?*

In no particular order and with no significance level, I can say with confidence that we mostly all agree the *G.O.A.T.* has to fill up stat sheets, be a winner, must have the clutch gene stuck in the *on position* at all times, has to be the alpha male of his/her time, has to have the defining moments (e.g., "11 … 10 … Jordan … Jordan the drive, hangs, fires, SCORES!" or "Blocked by James!"), has to have a long-lasting impact on and/or change the game, and most importantly, has to be that dude consistently with longevity. Some of it is also circumstantial – creating a dynasty or ending a championship drought will do it.

For those reasons, Charles Barkley, Patrick Ewing, Karl Malone, John Stockton, Carmelo Anthony, Chris Paul, etc. cannot even get into the *G.O.A.T.* conversation for their positions, let alone the actual *G.O.A.T.* conversation.

How could you possibly categorize Stockton and CP3 with Magic and Isaiah, or Chuck, Melo and the Mailman with Duncan and Bird, or Pat with Kareem and the Diesel? You can't because of the criteria mentioned. Are we in agreement on at least that much?

9

Thou Shall Covet the Rings - Jordan

Neither player reached the holy grail of NBA Championship victory and Finals MVP the way Magic did at age-20 in his rookie season in 1980, as he is one of a kind in this regard. Duncan and the Klaw are the second and fourth youngest to receive the honor, both at the age of 22 (Magic also won the award in 1982 at 22 years of age).[11]

Michael didn't win his first until his seventh season in the Association after his 28th birthday and LeBron didn't do the same until his ninth year in the league at age-27.[12] It is imperative to reiterate that championship pedigree starts with the franchise and luckily for Duncan and Kawhi, they were drafted by one of the best, if not the best, organizations in the game to a team with championship parts, while Magic was drafted by one of the top-two historic franchises in the game.

LeBron and Jordan were not as lucky, both being drafted by franchises that had never won a title and were in a state of turmoil and despair until they received their golden tickets. While the two did not win right away, it is important to understand the early years for each player.

The pre-Jordan Bulls saw only three All-Star selections[13] in the ten years before Jordan's arrival. After two consecutive Western Conference Finals appearances in June 1974 and 1975, respectively, mediocrity ensued. Seven of the next nine seasons saw the Bulls achieve sub-.500 records and two early playoff exits in the other two seasons.[14]

The mediocrity see-saw did not immediately tilt upon Jordan's arrival for the 1984-1985 campaign; however, the Bulls finally got their franchise player – no offense to Artie Gilmore and Chet Walker – and made the playoffs again. Jordan put up a more than stellar rookie campaign: started in all 82 games, led the Bulls in points, assists, rebounds, steals, free-throw percentage, player efficiency ratings, playing 38.3 minutes per game, averaging 28.2 points, while posting a 52/17/85 slash line, to go along with 6.5 rebounds, six assists, 2.4 steals and just under one block per game. He earned a starting spot on the Eastern Conference All-Star Team, Rookie of the Year honors, All-Rookie First Team and All-NBA Second Team selections. Most impressively, MJ finished sixth in MVP voting and received the second-most first-place votes.[15] From a statistical perspective, his numbers were the most comparable to those of that year's MVP, Larry Bird.

Speaking of Larry Bird, a fierce competitor, champion and one of the greatest to ever suit up in the NBA, he had extremely high praise for Jordan after going head-to-head and taking 41 points from the rookie, saying that he was the best player ever.[16] High praise from the reigning champion and MVP. Jordan was also featured on a *Sports Illustrated* cover in December of 1984, with the headline, *A Star is Born*.

Though the Bulls took a first-round exit in Jordan's rookie campaign, they were largely outmatched by a Bucks team boasting two All-NBA Second Team players and All-Stars in Sidney Moncrief and Terry Cummings, the latter of whom finished just ahead of Jordan in MVP voting, as well as Paul Pressey who was All-Defensive First Team, along with Moncrief, each of whom finished top-three in Defensive Player of the Year voting.[17]

Jordan did not disappoint in his playoff debut, averaging over 29 points, 8.5 assists and 5.8 rebounds to go along with just under three steals and one block in the four games.[18] If he accomplished nothing else as a rookie, he had put the NBA on notice.

Unfortunately, in the third game of his sophomore season, that notice went on hold when Jordan broke his foot, forcing him out of the next 64 games and causing Chicago to put a minutes restriction on their eventual franchise savior of 25 minutes per contest for the remainder of the season to the dismay of MJ and head coach, Doug Collins. MJ made it abundantly obvious that he wanted to make the playoffs even though further injury to his foot could have put his career in jeopardy. As we all know the legend of His Airness, this was the first glimpse we got of his renowned drive and competitiveness.

Where did this decision get him? A brief playoff appearance and a three-game sweep at the hands of the powerhouse Celtics who would go on to take the title again. Michael was highly regarded as the best player on the floor for the entire series. The Bulls unleashed MJ by releasing his post-injury restriction and what did he do? Mike averaged 44, six and six to go with two steals and a block in 45 minutes per game. Jordan also set a playoff record in a heartbreaking double-overtime loss in Game 2 by scoring 63 points.[19] Again, impressive from an individual standpoint, but not quite there.

MJ came back with a vengeance in the 1986-87 season, which is widely regarded as one of the most prolific offensive single-season outputs of all-time. Again, playing and starting all 82 games as he did in his rookie season, Jordan averaged 37, five and five to go with three steals and 1.5 blocks on 48% shooting. This would be his first of a record-10 scoring titles.[20] He also became the second player in NBA history to score 3,000 points in one season, the first player in NBA history with 200 steals and 100 blocks in a season, an odd feat for a 6'6" shooting guard. Magic won the MVP, with Jordan coming up just short, receiving the second-highest number of votes. Jordan also finished tied for eighth in DPOY voting, earned another All-Star appearance as a starter and earned a spot on the All-NBA First Team.[21]

Finally, His Airness backed his nickname by winning his first Slam Dunk contest[22] in one of the most mesmerizing showdowns in the contest's history.

Again, individually spectacular, but swept by the Celtics for the second consecutive year. The questions about Jordan being comparable to Bird and Magic were answered unanimously at this point. The rings were coveted by Jordan to say the least and losing killed Mike; he had one more mountain to climb before he reached the promised land.

The 1987-88 season was not much different from the past few for the Bulls – the main difference was a new villain, the *Bad Boys*. MJ had an unprecedented individual campaign and led the Bulls to the third seed in the Eastern Conference. Jordan racked up another scoring title with over 35 points per contest, the leader in steals per game with 3.2, All-Star Game MVP (this game featured 15 would-be Hall of Famers), and the unimaginable MVP and DPOY in the same year. Also added to Jordan moments was the 1988 Slam Dunk Contest title where he edged out 'Nique, which to this day is in the conversation of best of all-time.[23]

In addition to the obvious Hall of Fame checkboxes already mentioned, some modern numbers that wouldn't be created for some 20-plus years that Jordan put together during this campaign were a 37.1 player efficiency rating ("PER"), which was to-date the highest mark in the three point-era and Jordan's career-best, 21.2 win shares ("WS") and an 11.81 value over replacement player ("VORP"), which still remains the second-highest mark of all-time only to his 1988-89 VORP.[24]

That was the regular season. Jordan flipped the switch in the first round of the playoffs averaging about 45, five and five on 56% shooting[25] in a gentleman's sweep of Cleveland in the first round. The Bulls showed their young, upstart potential.

Enter the *Bad Boys*. One word to describe this series; *outmatched*. Like much of Michael's playoff experience to this point, the Bulls were a one-man show; many began to realize the Bulls had maxed out how far this roster would go. They needed a shake-up. Jordan averaged just under 28, nine and five with a solid slash of 49/33/79 in this five-game cakewalk for the Pistons.[26]

1988-89 was nearly a carbon copy of the previous year. Jordan still literally and figuratively had the taste of blood in his mouth from the beatdown the Pistons gave his Bulls in the prior campaign. His numbers, which are widely regarded as his best "all-around" single-season individual output, evidenced the chip on his shoulder. Jordan averaged 32.5, eight and eight with a tick under three steals and two ticks under one block on a 55/27/85 slash line during the regular season in which he missed only one game, averaging over 40 minutes per contest, his second consecutive year leading the league in minutes played. Something new, Jordan racked up 15 triple-doubles during the campaign, 11 of which came in the final 16 games of the season. Mike again compiled All-NBA First Team, All-Defensive First Team, All-Star selections and his third consecutive scoring title[27], leading the Bulls to the Eastern Conference Finals for a rematch with the *Bad Boys* after another first-round matchup with the Cavs in which he stuck a series-clinching jumper over Craig Ehlo and a 4-2 series win over the Knicks.

Unfortunately for the Bulls, the Pistons also had a bad taste in their mouths from the previous campaign where they fell in the Finals to Magic's Lakers. And so, we get to the infamous

Jordan Rules. What predicated this strategy implemented by Hall of Fame Coach Chuck Daly were two stellar regular season performance where MJ torched the Pistons' league-best defense for 59 and 61[28], with the Bulls winning both games; Daly vowed to never allow Jordan to tattoo his defense again.

It worked in the 1988 Eastern Conference Semis and was implemented yet again in the 1989 Eastern Conference Finals – Jordan was left battered and bloody on multiple occasions. After beating his initial assignment, he was lucky enough to have the likes of Bill Laimbeer, Rick Mahorn and John Salley ready to knock him out of the air if he dared enter the paint. Though the Bulls somehow took a 2-1 series lead in 1988, they fell three games in a row and bowed out to the Pistons for the second consecutive season and worse, watched them raise the O'Brien trophy.

Despite Jordan's 34.8 points, seven boards and 7.6 assists in the 1988 playoff run[29], it was just another season of coming up short. The pundits continued to question Jordan's ability to lead a championship team and the Bulls did what every franchise does to protect its star player when things don't go as planned – they fired the head coach for a new regime. Usually, this effort is futile – well, at least in my experience as a Knicks fan – but, it proved to be just what the Bulls needed. Phil Jackson and Tex Winter brought their *three-sided* approach to the big stage.

In 1988-1989, Michael was named to the All-NBA First Team, All-Defensive First Team and was a member of the All-Star Team. He won his fourth consecutive scoring title and led the league in steals for the second time in his career. By this point, MJ's numbers in the regular season aren't really worth stating as he recorded pretty much the same stats year-after-year. However, with the emergence of the triangle offense, his three-point shooting considerably spiked to 38%.[30]

MJ and the Bulls again finished second in the league behind the reigning Champion Pistons and waltzed through the first two rounds for a rematch Eastern Conference Finals with the *Bad Boys*. Move over Celtics-Lakers, this had become the premier rivalry in the Association.

The first four games were decided by less than ten points and split evenly. Michael was clearly the best player on the floor, averaging 36 per contest.[31] The home team won every game in the series, which worked in the Pistons favor as the number one seed in the conference; the Bulls were embarrassed in Game 7 and fell to the Pistons for the third consecutive year, though they inched closer and closer every time.

Through six seasons, one of which was almost a total loss, nobody had accumulated more individual hardware and accolades than His Airness, but unfortunately, six title-less runs don't earn you a spot on anybody's Mount Rushmore or in any *G.O.A.T.* conversation. That would all soon change for MJ, as the real legend of Mike had not even begun – the 1990s were upon us.

10

Thou Shall Covet the Rings - James

F ast forward to June 2003; we all watched LeBron shake the late-David Stern's hand on the stage in his all-white parachute ... I mean suit. LeBron's playing career started in a very Jordan-esque manner on October 29, 2003, giving the Sacramento Kings 25 points, nine assists, six rebounds and four steals.[32] He showed us the hype was real and has been putting up monster numbers ever since.

Like Jordan, he did not provide instant gratification to a franchise that hadn't seen any type of championship pedigree since the early-1990s when Jordan's Bulls discarded them in the conference finals. The year before LeBron's arrival, the Cavs won 17 games, which granted them *The Chosen One*.[33]

While the team had talent in Carlos Boozer, Ricky Williams, Darius Miles, Dajuan Wagner and Zydrunas Ilgauskas, the Cavs lacked veteran leadership that LBJ also couldn't provide as a 19-year-old. For this reason, the Cavs couldn't make the jump to the playoffs. The Rookie of the Year put up numbers that hadn't been seen by a rookie since, you guessed it, MJ's rookie campaign.

King James posted 20.9 points, 5.9 assists and 5.5 rebounds with 1.6 steals and 0.7 blocks, while shooting on a slash of 42/29/75.[34] Though LeBron's rookie year was statistically remarkable, he was left off of the Eastern Conference All-Star Team and All-NBA teams, which has unfortunately become a rite of passage for all rookies, no matter how well they distinguish themselves.

Maybe that was just what LeBron needed because year two was even more remarkable than his rookie campaign. Leading the league in minutes per game, LeBron averaged 27, seven and seven with two steals and slightly under one block on 47/35/75 shooting. He became only the 5th player to average 25, seven and seven at age-21 – wow. He also became an All-Star and was named to the All-NBA Second Team.[35]

Though the Cavs re-tooled by removing some players with problem reputations (Ricky Davis and Darius Miles) and surrounding James with a veteran presence in Eric Snow and Lucious Harris, the effort was not enough to get the Cavs into the playoffs with a 42-40 record.[36]

Enter Mike Brown. Let's be very clear Mike Brown did not have the same effect as Phil Jackson did on Jordan's Bulls, but he gave LBJ the freedom to run the offense as he wished and perhaps LeBron was getting comfortable in his own skin in his third year in the league. Danny Ferry continued his re-tool around LeBron by adding more veterans that could shoot and defend – Larry Hughes, Damon Jones and Donyell Marshall. The Cavs finished with a record of 50-32.[37]

LeBron continued on his tear, averaging just about 31, seven and seven with 1.6 steals and 0.7 blocks in 42.5 minutes per contest, shooting 48/34/74. He became the youngest player to average over 30 per game and one of only three players to average 31, 7 and 6. Another year as an All-Star and he made the All-NBA First Team.[38] Most importantly, he took the Cavs to the playoffs for the first time since 1997-98.

What did he do in his first playoff performance? What did you expect – a mere triple-double of 32, 11 and 11 in a win against a Wizards team led by Gilbert Arenas and Antawn Jamison. Followed that up with a 41-point performance in a pivotal Game 3, 45 in an overtime victory in Game 5 and 32 in a series-clinching overtime victory in Game 6. Not bad for your first postseason series.[39]

Unfortunately, the magic would run out. The Cavs drew the Pistons who had ended the Lakers' dynasty two years prior and lost in their repeat attempt in the prior campaign. Flip Saunders took a page out of Chuck Daly's *Jordan Rules* and used his superior defense to limit LeBron's production in the series. Let's use that term *limit* loosely. Only LeBron's scoring and shooting were down from its typical meteoric heights as he averaged 27 points, nine rebounds and six assists. He received essentially no help from his teammates in those departments as the rest of the team averaged only 54 points per contest.

After going up 3-2 in the series, the Cavs lost back-to-back games and were embarrassed at the Palace of Auburn Hills in Game 7 where they scored a measly 61 points, 27 by James.[40]

Like MJ, losing fueled LeBron. With essentially the same team in the next season, the LeBron-led Cavs finished 50-32, good enough for the second seed, second only to the same Pistons team that had ousted them in the 2006 Playoffs.

While LeBron's scoring was down, he still put up big numbers in the regular season, averaging 27 points, seven boards and six assists to go along with 1.6 steals and 0.7 blocks. He also saw another All-Star appearance and was All-NBA Second Team.[41]

The Cavs swept the Wizards in the first round and gave the aging Nets all they could handle in six games before a rematch with the Pistons in the conference finals. Defense prevailed in the first two games of the series, both games ending 79-76 in favor of the Pistons. LeBron would not accept the same fate leading his team to four straight victories and clinching a finals berth. One of his most memorable performances was the two-overtime thriller that was Game 5 on the road in the hostile Palace of Auburn Hills. The game was tight the entire way, with LBJ scoring 25 straight and 29 of the last 30 Cavalier points in the contest, leaving him with 48, nine rebounds and seven assists. There was no coming back for the aging Pistons in Game 6 and the Cavs had the unfortunate luck of facing Popovich's Spurs in one of the most mismatched Finals in NBA history.[42]

Tony Parker could not be stopped, prime Duncan, and excellent wing play from Michael Finley, Manu and Bruce Bowen, each of whom took turns stifling the King to a slash of 36/20/69. He still managed to produce; the games were close, but it only took 4 games to dismantle 22-year-old James and company.[43] The Cavs were not ready and went back to the drawing board after LeBron's fourth season in the league.

The Cavs brought in veterans Wally Szczerbiak, Joe Smith, Ben Wallace and also signed Delonte West, LeBron's step-father... sorry had to. LeBron won his first and only scoring title to date, while also averaging a tick under eight boards and seven assists to go along with 1.8 steals and 1.1 blocks on a slash line of 48/32/71 in another All-Star and All-NBA First Team season.[44] As the fourth seed, they once again discarded the Wizards in the first round, which led them to a newly assembled foe, the *Boston Three Party*.

Once again, Cleveland was no match for a prime Big Three to go along with a young maestro in Rajon Rondo and role players Posey, Perkins, Cassell, Tony Allen, Glen Davis, Eddie House and Leon Powe. Though severely outmatched, LeBron carried his team to Game 7, where home team advantage proved decisive.

The King dueled with the *Truth* and as always, the truth prevails. Pierce's 41 was enough to push back LeBron's 45. Though he averaged 26.7 in the series, his shooting slash line was 36/23/76.[45]

The questions began to swirl on *ESPN*, "Was LeBron clutch?" "Could he ever be as great as MJ and Kobe?" Sound familiar?

So, what was Cleveland's response to being so badly out-matched by its opponent? Mo Williams. No disrespect, but when we think of teams that needed to add a player to get over the hump, we're talking Pippen and Jordan, Shaq and Kobe, Parker and Duncan, Wade and Shaq, KG and Pierce. Did anyone actually think Mo Williams was Robin?

Well, it worked in the regular season at least. 66-16 and the overall best team in the Association. Williams averaged 18 per, while LeBron's output was as expected: 28, 7 and 7 with 1.7 steals and 1.1 blocks on stellar shooting, earning him his first MVP, an All-NBA First Team, All-Defensive First Team and All-Star selections.[46] Not bad for a 24-year-old.

How did the playoffs start, you ask? Let's see, eight games, eight wins.[47] Enter Orlando who just ousted the defending Champions in seven games. The Magic boasted a 23-year-old freak athlete claiming to be Superman and a solidly built team with excellent coaching.

For the first time in his career, LeBron had elevated his game in the playoffs from the regular season – this was no simple task, especially given the lack of supporting cast. As expected, LBJ led the Cavs in scoring in each of the series' games: 49, 35, 41, 37 and 25 for an average of 38.5 to go along with 8.3 boards and eight assists. The second-highest PER in playoff history was not enough to put away the Magic. Despite the overall stats, Game 7 was not his best work. LeBron shot on a slash of 40/25/64 and was a -12, whereas Dwight Howard came to play —he scored 40 to go along with 14 boards, four assists and one block.[48] Another year ended in disappointment for the

Chosen One, or was he?

Cleveland again attempted to re-tool and give LeBron some help. This time, Ferry answered with a long-past his prime Shaq, an Antawn Jamison that the Cavs had emasculated in playoff series after series and Anthony Parker, who is best known for being Candace's brother. The result was much of the same in the regular season. The Cavs were the overall best team in the Association again. LeBron averaged 29.7, 8.6 assists and 7.3 rebounds with 1.6 steals and one block on excellent all-around shooting, earning him his second consecutive MVP, an All-NBA First Team, All-Defensive First Team and All-Star selection.[49]

After a simple enough first-round series against the Bulls, the Cavs got a second crack at the C's. Though the Cavs had their best team in the LBJ era, the C's also made some major upgrades to their role players. It is still fair to say that LeBron was not on the better team, but his performance in the series did not do him any favors. Shooting numbers were down from the regular season and he averaged over four turnovers per game. The Cavs jumped to a 2-1 series lead but lost in six thanks to two, inexcusable home losses. James put forth a valiant effort in Game 6, but, once again, it was not enough.[50]

After seven short seasons, LeBron James made a decision, actually, *"The Decision"*.[51] In short, he decided that Cleveland could not put a team on the court to beat the powerhouses of the East, and famously took his talents to South Beach to form his own super team. Remember when Bruce Wayne left Gotham? [52] This is LeBron's version of that. The Kid from

Akron was on his way to Magic City.

After seven years of coming up short, LeBron seemed rejuvenated at the Heat's Welcome Party in the summer preceding the 2010-11 season at the American Airlines Center, "not two, not three, not four, not five, not six, not seven."[53]

Bold, arrogant, call it how you saw it, but something was clear – the *Kid from Akron* was now a villain to the other 29 franchises in the Association.

Many had picked the Heat to break the 1995-96 Bulls record of 72 wins, but they didn't even come close. While the Heat won their division, 58 wins were much lower than most projected for a team with three all-stars and a more than ample cast of veterans.[54] *"Paper never won a basketball game"* was never more applicable. It takes a while for a team with so many new pieces and focal points to mesh. In any event, Miami was the second seed in the East.[55]

Wade and Bosh had spectacular seasons as supporting actors to James, who put up another season with his usual numbers. He even managed to increase his field goal percentage to 51%.[56] He finished third in MVP voting to Derrick Rose and Dwight Howard, due to splitting votes with his teammate, D Wade, who finished seventh.[57] He was again an All-Star starter and All-NBA First Team and All-Defensive First Team.[58] There was only one thing left to do – bring home the hardware.

The Heat pushed aside Philly in round one and LeBron finally beat the Celtics in five games in round two. The MVP and

Chicago proved no match for the Heat either. LeBron made it back to the Finals for the first time since 2007 when he was embarrassed by the Spurs.[59]

Though he was not around for Shaq and D Wade's Finals victory, he was a part of the rematch between Miami and Dallas. Back to the theme of *paper*, LeBron and the Heat were heavily favored to win the Finals and they had the team to do it, for sure.

Well… let's just call the Mavs *"scissors"*. The Mavs took away the Heat's home field and lost it right back in Game 3. The Heat wound up losing not four, not five, but all of games four, five and six to the Mavs. See what I did there? One of the best team performances in Finals history. I expect a *30 for 30* on that Mavs team soon. The architect, Dwayne Casey, put LeBron James in Guantanamo for this series with unbelievable schematics and stifled the best run and gun team in the league with DeShawn Stevenson (who was a part of the Wizards' teams who were bested year-after-year by LeBron's Cavs) and a hobbled Shawn Marion.[60]

LeBron did not deliver on the biggest stage. James' scoring average of 17.8 points per game during the Finals represented a nine-point drop from his 26.7 points per game average during the regular season, the lowest such drop-off in league history. His 60% free throw percentage was also far below his season and career averages.[61] Both Wade and Bosh attempted to pick up the slack, but Dirk and Jason Terry were too much to handle offensively. Yes, that's what I said. Now, LeBron had no excuses and once again did not show up. Luckily, he had an extended offseason for some much-needed soul searching due to the lockout.

Let's recap on the kids that took the league by storm. Both players had eerily similar circumstances and tremendous individual success. The question marks were also similar. In the Summer of 1990, say that you had claimed to be from the future and told the talking heads, "hey, give the Jordan kid a break he's gonna have six rings in six chances," or in the Summer of 2011, "LeBron will go to the Finals for damn near the entire decade," how would you be perceived?

Greatness was established before either player won a ring, no arguments there. G.O.A.T.-status wasn't revealed until the demons were fought off and the commissioner passed along the hardware. But, let's make one thing crystal clear, the losing years elevated each player unquestionably. Losing can either make you a loser or it can make you a winner.

IV

Climb to the Prime

11

Make Your Case – Jordan's Defining Years

osing was important to mention and that will be abundantly obvious in later segments and discussions. The winning is obviously the reason we are having this discussion and we will get into specific moments and seemingly insurmountable barriers that were torn down to achieve it, but I don't see a point in going into the same level of detail for the "prime" years that brought out the inner *G.O.A.T.*, so I'll keep it as brief as possible.

We'll break Jordan down into pre- and post-baseball. In his pre-baseball three-peat, Jordan accumulated two MVPs, three scoring titles, one steals leader, three All-NBA First Team selections, three All-Defensive First Team selections, and above all else, three Finals MVPs. During these three seasons, he averaged 31 points, six assists, six rebounds, two steals and one block, while missing only six of 246 contests. He shot 52% from the field, 31% from three-point land and 84% from the free-throw line during this span.[62]

After sweeping the Pistons, in his first Finals in 1991 against Magic's Lakers, Jordan averaged 31 points, 11 assists and seven boards with three steals and one block, elevating his all-around game and doing what needed to be done to catch the elusive ring he had been chasing his entire career.[63]

Jordan and the Bulls remained hungry and defended their title against the Blazers in 1992 after tough matchups with the Knicks and Cavs. Jordan broke the single postseason record for total points and three-pointers in a Finals' game with six in Game 1 during this championship run, but most importantly, took care of Drexler and the Blazers in six games to secure his second consecutive championship and Finals MVP.[64]

Before the three-peat attempt, Jordan led the historic Dream Team to Olympic Gold in 1992 and still had the motivation to capture a third straight ring and Finals MVP in 1993 against the Phoenix Suns. Before getting there, the Bulls swept the Hawks and Cavs before going down 0-2 to the Knicks in the Eastern Conference Finals. Hope was short-lived for the Knicks as the Bulls won the next four, with Jordan recording a triple-double in Game 5 before returning home to clinch another Finals berth against the Suns and MVP Charles Barkley.[65] Was it fair to say Jordan took Barkley's MVP personally? I don't know, how does 41 per contest to go along with nine boards and six assists sound? The 41 per game in the Finals holds as a record to this day.[66]

We can talk about the Birmingham Barron's later on when we address hypotheticals, but for now, yes, Air Jordan retired on top of his game after a three-peat, much to the dismay of just about everyone except for the Knicks and Magic.

The return in the 45 was epic, but uneventful in *G.O.A.T.*-speak. The *double-nickel* performance against the Knicks was enough to make everyone forget the brief absence from the game. Ultimately, Shaq and Penny were the only ones to bring down Jordan in the 1990s. Did that fuel him?[67]

1995-96: new pieces and more chemistry. The Bulls posted a record of 72-10, talk about an act of vengeance.[68] Individually, Jordan got back the MVP, scoring title, both All-NBA and Defensive First teams and to put everyone back on notice, an All-Star MVP for fair measure. Oh wait, almost forgot – once again NBA Champion and Finals MVP.[69] In the playoffs, Jordan reminded the Knicks who their daddy was, let Shaq and Penny know that lightning doesn't strike twice and then beat up Payton, Kemp and company for a fourth ring.[70]

1996-97 was pretty much a carbon copy, except Jordan allowed Glen Rice to take home the All-Star Game MVP. Similar to when Barkley took home the MVP in 1993, Karl Malone won the award in 1997; Jordan would have the last laugh again as the Finals MVP and holder of a full hand of rings.[71]

The turmoil within the Bulls organization was intensely documented during the 1997-98 campaign, as we saw in *The Last Dance*.[72] Without Scottie for parts of the season, Jordan secured the last of his All-NBA and Defensive First Team selections, scoring titles, MVP trophies and All-Star Game MVPs.[73] Once again, the Bulls marched to the Finals, almost mundane at this point in a rematch with the Jazz. The Bulls were Vegas dogs in the Finals for the first time since 1991 or 1993, depending on who your bookie was. After a junkyard dog series that went seven games against Indiana, the Bulls dynastic legacy depended on this series.[74]

Fast forward to Game 6. If you watched it live, your photographic memory is envisioning it now. Easy bucket with just over 30 seconds left to create the two-for-one, clamps down, double the post, snatch the rock from the Mailman, then, *The Last Shot*. Right-to-left crossover, a little love tap on Bryon Russell's ass, making him the *bull* and Jordan the *matador* (pun intended), stop on a dime, elevate, bottoms up. Whether it is in your driveway or in a Finals clinching moment on the last shot of your career, that is the way you want your last shot of the day to go. Six rings, Six Finals MVPs. BAAAAAAA (goat noise).

While Jordan burst onto the scene in the 1980s, he will be immortalized for the 1990s, which is the best decade in the history of all decades (relax, but actually).

12

Make Your Case – James' Defining Years

L eBron's chronology is not as linear as Jordan's. For that reason, we'll split between Miami and Cleveland. For now, we won't consider his Lakers tenure, as at the time of writing, he has only participated in one injury-plagued season. Again, I will keep it as brief as possible.

With Miami, LBJ won two MVPs, two Finals MVPs, four All-NBA First Team, three All-Defensive First Team, one All-Defensive Second Team and four All-Star selections. During his tenure with the Heat, he averaged 27 points, eight rebounds and seven assists, to go along with nearly two steals and one block per game on 55% from the field, 37% from three and 76% from the line, with similar numbers in the playoffs in each of his four seasons with the club.[75]

The Heat finished a strike-shortened 2012 season with a 46-20 record and went on to beat a young, Thunder squad, who wasn't prepared for the beast.[76] James' Game 6 in the Eastern

Conference Finals in the Boston Garden is one of his all-time playoff performances. On the brink of elimination in hostile territory, he scored 45 to go along with 15 boards and five assists on 19 of 26 shooting.[77] He was unconscious and followed up with another spectacular performance, willing his team to the Finals. Lebron and company finished off the Thunder in Game 5 of the Finals with James recording a 26, 11 and 13 triple-double.[78]

James followed up his double-MVP performance by repeating his individual and team accomplishments and accolades in 2013, thanks to the help of a new teammate, Ray Allen, who was lured over from the Celtics.[79]

After a tough, grind-it-out series with the Pacers in the Eastern Conference Finals, the Heat met a more formidable opponent in the Spurs in the Finals. Down 3-2, the Spurs had the lead in Game 6 with 30 seconds to go. The morning headlines were already being written with LeBron and the Heat being labeled as choke artists. The trophy was already being prepared for the post-game presentation. While Bosh and Allen are largely credited with saving the day, in that memorable tap out to the corner three, James did his part and was the main reason why the Heat were in the position to tie and then win in overtime, both for good and bad.

King James began the fourth quarter with 11 consecutive points, but then missed a lightly contested jumper, a free throw and turned the ball over three times in five minutes. He then pulled the Heat within two with 20 seconds to go on a three-pointer. Kawhi, who had a masterful coming out party in locking up

LeBron as much as one possibly could early in the series, missed one of two free throws. The King pulled up for three, missed and the Bosh to Allen tap and corner three forced OT, where the Heat edged out the Spurs.[80]

LeBron could not be stopped in Game 7, finishing with 37, 12 and four en route to his second consecutive title and Finals MVP.[81]

After cruising to the top seed in the Eastern Conference, the Heat took only three losses in discarding the Hornets, Nets and Pacers on their way to a rematch with the Spurs.[82] One year had passed, but the majority of the Heat's roster looked like they were in a time machine and came back 20 years older, including 2013's hero, Ray Allen. The Flash, D Wade, showed signs of wear and tear on his body and Bosh looked like he didn't belong on the court at times. Outside of LeBron's 28 per game, nobody on the squad averaged more than 15, reminiscent of his days in Cleveland.[83]

Then there were *cramps*. In Game 1, LeBron famously missed the fourth quarter with cramps. In that same fourth quarter, the Spurs outscored the Heat 36-17, resulting in a 15-point win. In Game 2, LeBron had his best performance with 35, nine in the fourth to sneak out of San Antonio with a two-point win, eliminating the Spurs' home-court advantage.[84]

The Spurs were too much for the Heat to handle in the next three games winning by an average margin of 19. While LeBron had excellent numbers, the Spurs did an amazing job of containing him when it mattered most, in the fourth quarters.[85]

Just like that South Beach 'Bron was no more. He returned to Cleveland, perhaps tired of playing the villain, perhaps with the winning experience he needed to bring his hometown team their long-awaited championship, or perhaps knowing the Cavs had what he needed in a supporting cast, only he knows the real reason.

In four more seasons with the Cavs, LeBron added to his Finals resume with another ring, an all-time performance in a losing effort in which he nearly won a Finals MVP. From a regular season perspective, he added four more All-Star and All-NBA First Team selections, as well as the All-Star Game MVP in 2018.[86]

In his return season, the Cavs were finally able to form a Big Three for LeBron, with the other two parts being Kyrie Irving and Kevin Love. The supporting cast wasn't as good as it was for LeBron in his two titles with Miami, but more adept than his former Cleveland teams were. The Cavs finished second in the East, dropping two games in the Eastern Conference Semis to the Bulls, but sweeping Boston and conference leader, Atlanta, in the other two series, leading to LeBron's fifth consecutive Finals appearance.[87]

Unfortunately, Kevin Love and Kyrie Irving were unable to suit up for this series and LeBron was forced to lean on Timofey Mozgov and Matthew Dellavedova in their respective places. After going up 2-1, the Cavs really stood no chance and ultimately succumbed to a new rival. Despite the shortcomings of the team, LeBron did what he could in 46 minutes per game – not a typo – 36 points, 13 rebounds and eight assists on a horrendous shooting slash of 40/31/69, but one could only do so much when being the only offensive option.[88]

2015-2016 can be summed up very briefly: *Did the Dubs really blow a three-one lead?* Yes, they did. Not worth mentioning the season because LeBron and the Cavs finished first and left the east in their wake, as would be expected.[89]

After two games against the 73-9, record-breaking Warriors, it looked a lot like another Finals loss for the King and the Cavs, but Cleveland stormed back with a 30-point blowout in Game 3.[90] Game 4 was a loss for Cleveland, but the bigger loss was losing Draymond Green to suspension for, well, not being composed and getting baited by who else, LeBron. It is also important to note that Tristan Kardashian … err … Thompson called LeBron's manhood into question. The King responded in Game 5 with 41, 16 and seven, followed by 41, eight and 11 in Game 6. Momentum had swung as the series was leveled at three.

Game 7 in the Bay was one of the best Finals games I have ever seen. Back and forth, everything you could ask for and more. Would LBJ shrink or defer, or would he earn his stripes in the G.O.A.T. conversation? Let's not forget, the Warriors were 73-9 and unstoppable in the regular season.

He showed up when he had often been criticized for not. In the fourth quarter, LBJ scored 11, including back-to-back three-point plays. Kyrie, in the role of Robin, ultimately took the glory with the final shot, making him an overnight superstar, but *Blocked by James* is still the greatest play in Finals history, better than *The Shot*.

The way he closed the gap on Iguodala and beat the ball to the backboard as to avoid a goaltending call is just one of those things you cannot explain and sometimes question its reality even though you saw it happen. People still owe me money from this comeback that I called at 3-1; shame game to *Carlo's Pizzeria* on Metropolitan Avenue in Queens for not paying their debt and calling me crazy for betting them. The pizza's pretty good; I'll let it slide.

But, did his third ring and Finals MVP come at a hefty cost towards his legacy? KD would arrive in Oakland and that did not bode well for LeBron in the next two years. Not even worth talking about what happened in those two finals, other than J.R. Smith being J.R. Smith. Who knows what could've happened if they stole Game 1 in 2017?

Taking out Goliath surely put LBJ in the conversation, but on the surface, based on what we have brought to the table, there's really no conversation to be had. Jordan was *the* apex predator in the Finals being 6-0. James, for the most part, was known to crumble in the Finals at 3-6. We are going to give LeBron the benefit of the doubt and take a much deeper dive because records and intangibles do not mean everything.

Also, let's mention that just because Jordan was undefeated in the Finals didn't mean he never lost. He lost his fair share as well. If Finals wins were the only thing that mattered, we would have to include Big Shot Bob, Robert Horry, but he was not *that dude*. And also, we have to take into consideration competition. The 1950s and '60s Celtics centered around Bill Russell were unbelievable, but they didn't face the competition we see in the modern game. Stay tuned; it's about to get way deeper than this conversation goes at your barber.

V

Myth Busting

13

Competition – The Fallacy of Accountants vs Athletes

For starters, I want to make it known that as a CPA, I take extreme offense to this notion that MJ played against accountants and gym teachers; some of us can ball out. Personal vendettas aside, this is a clear fallacy and I will happily provide the evidence to debunk it.

The first chapter clearly goes into the topic of competition, so I won't repeat myself. To say that the NBA doesn't change from decade to decade would be a lie. Just take a look at the box scores in the 1990s vs the box scores in today's game! Clearly, something has changed.

If you don't believe me, take a look at the mysterious line that was added to the court in 1979 to welcome Magic and Bird. It took many years to be utilized and only until very recently (about 30-35 years after its initial adoption) have we seen what we believe to be its full potential and importance to the game. How about the euro step, illegal defense, foul tactics and other late-game strategies, small ball, etc.?

There will always be intricacies and analytics that change the game as we know it. But, the one constant is *competition*. Teams will always give their opposition great competition in this league. While it is nearly impossible to compare teams and players that never played against each other, we can measure competition.

Does today's game have better athletes than in the 1980s and 1990s? As a whole, most certainly, but were there athletes from the 1980s and 1990s that could unquestionably hang with, if not embarrass modern-day players' athleticism? *See* Dr. J, Darryl Dawkins, Dominique Wilkins, Clyde Drexler, Shawn Kemp, and many others.

It is important to remember that athleticism doesn't necessarily translate into better basketball players, now or then. So sure, would Russell Westbrook and Derrick Rose have been killers in the 1980s? But would Chris Paul be even better than both of them in that era? Very difficult to say either way.

Let's flip to the other side of the token; think about deadeye, limitless shooters who played in the 1980s and 1990s. Take Larry Bird. In Bird's career, he attempted just over 1,700 three-pointers, shooting at a 38% clip.[91] By comparison, Brook Lopez has taken over 1,500 in his last four seasons, shooting 34% from beyond.[92] Imagine in the primitive times of the arc, had teams understood its value – how many points would Bird have averaged? Think about how defenses would have been impacted and how easily he would have been able to get to his mid-range and into the paint with teams running him off the line the way teams run the Splash Bros off the line. Imagine if there was no hand checking and patty cake fouls were called. Would Bird have gotten to the line as easily as James Harden?

The answer is simple – *we will never know*. So, I challenge people that say, "So-and-so would average 50 in the 1980s and 1990s," to ask themselves, "How many would Bird average in today's game? Mark Price? Drazen Petrovic? Tim Legler? Steve Kerr?" And it's not just shooting; so many aspects of the game have changed. Think about if a young Shaq played for a run and gun team with shooters like today's Bucks? Would he not have a similar, if not better line than Giannis? Would James Harden average nine free throw attempts per game in the 1980s or 1990s with the differences in officiating and hand-checking?[93]

My point is that the argument goes both ways, but it has the same answer no matter which side of the fence you are on – there's no way of knowing. What we do know is that the competition was fierce and oppositions gave one another all they could handle. Let's see if we can measure the level of postseason competition faced by both players in our conversation.

14

The "Accountants"

For purpose of this conversation, I will name the main "accountants" that MJ and the Bulls lost to in the postseason to refute the outlandish hypothesis posed by those with limited knowledge of the game. I will get into his road to losing and/or winning a championship later on.

In 1985, the Bulls lost to the 59-23 Milwaukee Bucks in the first round of the playoffs. This team was represented by Terry Cummings, Sidney Moncrief and Paul Pressey. Cummings and Sidney Moncrief were All-NBA Second Team selections that year, while Moncrief and Pressey were All-Defensive First Team selections. Terry Cummings was an All-Star and finished fifth in MVP voting, receiving two first-place votes. Sidney Moncrief finished eighth in the same voting, while also being an All-Star.[94]

Cummings was also named Rookie of the Year in the 1982-83 season.[95] Moncrief was a five-time All-Star from 1982-86, All-NBA First Team selection in 1982-83, All-NBA Second Team selection in 1982, 1984-86, two-time Defensive Player of the Year in 1983-84, All-Defensive First Team selection in 1983-86, All-Defensive Second Team selection in 1982 and an NBA Hall of Famer.[96]

In 1986 and 1987, Michael and the Bulls were swept by the Celtics. These Celtics teams included Larry Bird, Kevin McHale, Robert Parish, Bill Walton, Dennis Johnson and Danny Ainge, all of whom were Hall of Famers, except for Danny Ainge, an All-Star. In both years, Bird, McHale and Parish were All-Stars. Amongst this group were 36 All-Star selections, 17 All-NBA Team selections, 20 All-Defensive Team selections, three Sixth Men of the Year, four MVPs, 16 Championship Rings and four Finals MVPs among many other accolades and distinctions.[97] [98]

As we have alluded to in earlier chapters, Jordan and the Bulls were owned by the Bad Boys from 1988-90. These teams consisted of Isiah Thomas, Adrian Dantley, Joe Dumars, Dennis Rodman, Bill Laimbeer, Mark Aguirre, Rick Mahorn, John Salley and Vinnie Johnson. These Pistons teams weren't as decorated as the Celtics teams to which the Bulls fell; they only had four Hall of Famers in Zeke, Dantley, Dumars, and Rodman. Those mentioned were named to 31 All-Star teams and 12 All-NBA teams and 14 All-Defensive teams! Additionally, there were two All-Star Game MVPs, two Scoring Champs and obviously, two Finals MVPs.[99][100][101]

There is only one more team to mention and I do so with an asterisk as the Jordan-led Bulls had a playoffs series record of 30-7. The asterisk goes next to the 1994-95 Orlando Magic led by Shaq, Penny and Horace Grant, complimented by Nick Anderson, Dennis Scott and Brian Shaw. The asterisk comes as Jordan only played 17 regular-season games and a first-round series this year due to his baseball quest.[102] Jordan was clearly not the same player in 1994-95, but it was a loss, nevertheless.

This team's Big Three are responsible for 20 All-Star selections, 17 All-NBA team selections, seven All-Defensive team selections, two scoring titles, three All-Star Game MVPs, one MVP and three Finals MVPs.[103] Granted, most of these accolades were accumulated by Shaq, pre-injury Penny was destined for greatness and Horace Grant played an integral role on four championship teams. Obviously the Magic were not nearly as dominant as the previously mentioned Celtics and Pistons, but a formidable opponent nevertheless.

One thing is certain – MJ did not lose to accountants. I am hoping we can all agree on that much. I would be remiss to not mention the leaders of the competition that ushered Jordan to his seven postseason exits. After all, only 12 coaches and 10 organizations have won titles since Jordan came into the league. The coaches of these teams were Don Nelson, K.C. Jones, Chuck Daly, and Brian Hill, all of whom except for Brian Hill (who was granted wonderful gifts by the Lottery Gods) were Hall of Famers and Champions while at the helm!

Okay, so how about the *accountants* he beat? We won't go through the 30 playoffs series wins Jordan and the Bulls racked up, but let's just talk through the series in which the Bulls were underdogs and/or a lower seed.

In 1989, the Bulls were the sixth seed and beat a Cavs team that went 57-25 in the full five games, clinching the series in Cleveland on a pull-up jumper that Jordan hit on Craig Ehlo with 6 seconds to go. That's the short of it, but let's dive into the background of this series.

The Bulls were on the rise going into the 1989-90 season. I would liken this season to a major company selling pre-initial public offering shares. The big IPO was imminent and bandwagoners (or the *investors*) were expected to be cashing in as the Celtics' years of prosperity were ending fast. While the Pistons were certainly seen as on the rise, they were not expected to be a long-term replacement for the Celtics' dynasty. Coming off of a fifty-win season in the previous campaign, addition of big man, Bill Cartwright, from the Knicks in exchange for Charles Oakley and the maturity of athletic frontcourt mates, Grant and Pippen, everyone expected the Bulls to separate themselves.

This was a clear case of expectations versus reality because the Cavs took off, winning 57 games, defeating the Bulls six times during the 1988-89 campaign! The last of those six came on the final game of the season in Chicago; Cleveland beat the Bulls' starters while benching their own. Yikes! Round one was not looking good for Chicago. On the eve of the playoffs, some Chicago sports columnists even went as far as saying that MJ would never win a title – I bet Jordan has those newspaper clippings saved in a scrapbook somewhere.

Mark Price, Larry Nance, and Brad Daugherty were All-Stars, and Horace Grant started in the playoffs for the first time.

Not to mention, Ron Harper, then before knee surgery, was regarded as Jordan's athletic equal. Lenny Wilkens also had the credentials as head coach. Most national observers had the Cavs in a sweep.

Wilkens was widely criticized for multiple tactics in this series and Price's injury that forced him out of Game 1 lingered throughout the series. Ultimately, it was the Bulls' hounding defense that led them to victory; oh, and MJ's famous pull-up over Ehlo. This was Jordan's most iconic playoff moment to-date.

The underdog run was not done there. The Knicks were next on the docket, having won 52 games this season. The first four games of the series had much wider margins than those of the Cavs series, which were all decided by less than eight points. But, the Knicks, coached by Rick Pitino and led by Big Pat, Mark Jackson, Gerald Wilkins, Johnny Newman and Oak Tree, with a solid bench of veterans Sidney Green, Trent Tucker and Kiki Vandeweghe, buckled down for Games 5 and 6, losing the latter by two on MJ's 40 points, 10 assists, five rebounds and four blocks on 64% shooting.[104]

Fast forward to the conference semi's in 1990 against the Sixers who were the Eastern Conference's second seed that year, led by the Round Mound of Rebound, Chuck. While he tends to be a walking meme nowadays, Barkley was a force and entering his prime. Chuck averaged 25, 11 and four with All-Star and All-NBA selections.[105] More than adequately accompanied by Johnny Dawkins, Hersey Hawkins, Rick Mahorn and Mike Gminksi, Barkley's Sixers stood no match to Jordan and the

Bulls on the hardwood, where games are actually played; they were discarded in four games.

The Bulls were once again slight dogs in the 1991 and 1993 NBA Finals. The *accountants* they faced in those series were none other than Magic, Sam Perkins, A.C. Green, Vlade Divac and Elden Campbell in the former and Chuck, Kevin Johnson, Dan Majerle, Danny Ainge and Tom Chambers in the latter. I hope that we have all seen what Magic and Chuck have done as athletic marvels on a basketball court, but if you haven't had the chance, please watch some highlight tapes on KJ and Chambers.

If I had to liken KJ to somebody from the modern game from a skills and athleticism perspective, he would fall between young Deron Williams and Derrick Rose. While he was not quite as explosive as Rose, he had similar size and tendencies and I would argue his playmaking and shooting were more comparable to a Utah Deron Williams, but do your own research and watch this 6'1" maestro cut up some ankles and hammer it home on a big waiting as the last line of defense.

Tom Chambers is one of only two eligible players to have scored 20,000 points without being elected to the Hall of Fame.[106] The 6'10" forward is most famously remembered for the absolute sledgehammer he gave to Mark Jackson off a dime from KJ. On a fast break, Chambers received the rock, took one stride inside the free-throw line, kneed Mark Jackson in the chin on the outskirts of the restricted semi-circle, cocked it back with two hands, elbows and nose at the rim and hammered it home. While Chambers stereotypically looked like an accountant, I don't know many accountants who could pull off a move like that. Please find the clip and see for yourself.

Before seeing the Suns in the Finals that year, the Bulls were also a lower seed and dog to the Knicks in the Eastern Conference Finals. That squad featured Big Pat, Starks, Oakley, Mase and Doc Rivers. A fair comparison for Starks from an athletic standpoint would probably be young D Wade or Bradley Beal, while Doc's athletic comparison could be Avery Bradley or his son, Austin.

Mase and Draymond are very much alike. Pat and Oakley really don't translate into the modern game to make a comparison, but Pat's style was ahead of his time as an athletic, shooting center and Oakley's toughness and strength would be matched by few in today's game. Again, these guys were not necessarily Russell Westbrook's and Blake Griffin's, but no slouches by any means.

The last time Jordan's Bulls would be an underdog to odds-makers was in the last year of the second three-peat to Indiana in the conference finals. While I will lead with the fact that this team was not a team with certified speed demons, leapers and handlers that would be seen on the *And1 Mixtape Tour*, this team was exceptional and, in my opinion, probably a top playoff opponent that the Jordan-era Bulls beat after the 1993 Knicks and Suns and 1997 Jazz. The Pacers were comprised of Reggie Miller, Mark Jackson, Dale Davis, Chris Mullin, Rik Smits, Antonio Davis, Travis Best and Jalen Rose.

What a great transition into the teams and defensive matchups that LeBron has faced in the Finals. In 2007, LeBron was famously outmatched by the San Antonio Spurs in a lackluster performance. The best athlete on this team is difficult to identify and not for a plethora of options, rather a dearth. Was it Manu or TP? The Spurs' average age was nearly 31 and the youthful players were Parker and Beno Udrih, neither of whom were known for athleticism. The wings of Michael Finley, Bruce Bowen and Brent Barry were pretty good athletes in their day, but not at this time in their respective careers; the same can be said for Robert "Big Shot Bob" Horry. Duncan wasn't a slouch of an athlete, but there's a reason his nickname was "The Big Fundamental" and not "Air Walker".

Next up, 2011 Dallas and quite possibly the least athletic team to win a ring in the modern era. Based on the names I am about to mention, this might seem like a farce but bear with me.

I don't think I will get any backlash by naming Dirk (32) who was hobbled and ill for portions of the series, J Kidd (37), Peja, and Brian Cardinal. Brendan Haywood and Ian Mahinmi combined for less than 20 minutes per contest. Haywood was past his athletic and basketball prime at this point, while Mahinmi was a mobile rim running big, but by no means a Dwight Howard. Then, Jason Terry and J.J. Barea. Both were extremely quick, great shooters and penetrators, but to call either a plus-athlete in the NBA would be a stretch and a half.

Tyson Chandler was for sure a plus-athlete at this stage in his career and an anchor on defense; he played an integral role as the last line of defense to stop the King. Finally, let's mention the two players who spent most of the series guarding LBJ, Shawn Marion and DeShawn Stevenson. Marion was a superior athlete with Phoenix but, at 32 and after sustaining multiple injuries to his back and knees throughout his career, was not nearly the athlete he was with the Suns.

Still an able-body, tremendous defender and rebounder, Marion did a great job on LeBron when Stevenson wasn't clamping him up. In a recent interview, when asked about guarding LeBron, he recalled the 2011 Finals, "It's hard, he's a hell of a player, very talented so it's always tough. But you know, with that team and the way my mentality was, we just had that team that we wasn't going to stand for anything."[107]

While Stevenson was a great athlete, he didn't measure up physically to James and I do not think anyone can disagree with that outside of a mental institution.

It is important to note at this point that LeBron was not bothered by athleticism in his first two finals appearances, but rather he was worn down by a tough, gritty team defense. No one particular player deserves the full credit for stifling the King. Popovich, Carlisle and Dwayne Casey deserve the credit as architects, not just for their respective series, quite frankly for how many teams down the road attempted to guard LeBron. The difference though was the execution and team buy-in from two stellar organizations.

The most athletic team that LeBron faced in the Finals was the 2012 Oklahoma City Thunder, who were bluntly outmatched from an experience perspective. Russ, KD, Ibaka, Harden and company are all plus plus-athletes. Even in this series, the task of guarding LBJ was split, but James overwhelmed the young

Thunder, even with all that youth and athleticism.

The Heat went back-to-back in 2013, playing a Spurs team with the same core and totally different supporting cast from six years prior in what turned out to be one of the most amazing NBA Finals in this millennium. The Spurs retooled and added one of the great NBA athletes in Kawhi Leonard, who played LeBron very well in the series, which was ultimately salvaged by Ray Allen's clutch factor. Diaw, Ginobli and Danny Green rounded out the council of James' covers in both 2013 and 2014. As the coin flips, the Spurs got their revenge in 2014 with a transcendent defensive performance from the 22-year old finals MVP.

LeBron and Cleveland then lost the next three of four Finals to the Warriors dynasty. It could be argued that the Warriors with KD are the most dynamic, athletic finals foe of LeBron, but the Cavs were clearly outmatched in all three of these Finals except for 2016 where LeBron was covered predominantly by Dray, Iggy, Harrison Barnes and at times, Livingston and Klay. Again, it was not so much size and athleticism that bothered LeBron, but the ability to switch on the perimeter and help in the middle from Bogut when LeBron beat his man. Another full-team scheme was required to stop the King. LBJ prevailed in 2016 after trailing 3-1. If Draymond doesn't get suspended and miss Game 6, who knows what LeBron's legacy looks like?

So, let's recap. Did Jordan beat up on *accountants*? Would King James have destroyed the 1990s competition that Jordan faced or the 1980s competition that MJ got destroyed by? Would Jordan have killed or been killed in the 2000s or

2010s? We cannot definitively say, but what we can conclude is this: *athleticism is only part of the Championship pedigree and it is not even necessarily an integral part.* More important than athleticism is the team and the system, as well as skill and determination. The intangibles separate championship contenders from champions. The Celtics and Pistons of the 1980s and early 1990s had the same composition as the Mavs, Spurs and Warriors that LeBron faced in that a team defensive approach was key, talent was never lacking and strong veteran presence from the coaching staff and role players were the x-factors. Thus, I have presented the *fallacy of the accountants.* However, we are not done with the competition conversation.

15

Competition – Did Mike End the Eastern Conference?

As we have already documented, the East was the superior conference in the 1990s. That doesn't just mean the champions either; I am talking about the perennial problems that were the Knicks, the Magic, the Pacers, the Heat, etc. No road to the Finals is easy, but some are easier than others. This is not to say that the West was bad in the 1990s either. Portland, Utah, San Antonio and Houston were great for major parts of the decade.

Early on, LeBron had to face tough Pistons, Nets, Celtics and Magic teams with Cleveland. The Eastern Conference talent when James was with the Heat seemed to drop off significantly, but it was more a matter of Miami being so good. The Celtics, Bulls and Pacers teams LeBron and the Heat collided with were not measly opponents by any measure.

Not sure if the same could be said of the East during LeBron's second stint with the Cavs. During this time, the city of Toronto was renamed *LeBronto*, the Hawks were not such great birds of prey, but rather the prey to LeBron year-after-year and that whole Boston-LeBron rivalry from the decade prior was not such a rivalry anymore.

By this point, was the Eastern Conference weaker than it was in the 1990s and early 2000s? Was it the junior circuit to the Western Conference? Absolutely, but can we hold LeBron accountable for that? *Yes, but in a good way.* He was so dominant that free agents decided to move out west as they felt they had a better shot at a Finals appearance that way and Eastern Conference franchises decided to rebuild in efforts to outlast LeBron's reign over the East. This is so abundantly obvious that the structure of the All-Star Game was changed as the talent pool from the West was so much deeper than that of the East.

I said LeBron was to blame for this and I think that is a fair statement due to his *greatness*, but we cannot hold that *against* him. Playoff basketball is playoff basketball; LeBron, like Jordan, was physically battered and mentally drained from his title runs, both successful and unsuccessful. That is evident in both players' follicular shortcomings. While LeBron made it seem like a waltz through the East at times, Jordan did as well, and I can guarantee both players will say it required their respective all to do so. I can also guarantee that teams they swept will go on record as saying they didn't lay down for them to step over.

Mike, nor LeBron, ended either conference. There are so many factors that go into franchise success that don't even have to do with basketball. The market of the franchise, the weather, the state income tax, the lottery balls, etc. No one basketball player can end competition in a particular conference, not even the greatest player. When was the last time Charlotte or Oklahoma City was able to lure a top tier free agent away from a bigger market? $100 million in Miami and Houston is way more than $100 million in New York as far as income taxes go. These factors all play a far more important role than a player ever could in dictating the power index of the league. I have now given you the *fallacy of the strong versus weak Eastern Conference*.

16

The Oscar for Best Performance in a Supporting Role

Much of this debate is centered around super teams, dynasties, ring-chasing veterans, etc. So, who had the better squads? Were LeBron's early Cleveland teams really as bad as they're made out to be? Were MJ's Bulls teams that far superior to everyone else?

Well, let's start off this way; no bad team has ever won an NBA championship. I'll say it again; no bad team has ever won an NBA championship. The grueling nature of an 82-game season followed by a 16-team playoff tree almost guarantees that the best team will come out victorious, save for injuries. It's nearly impossible to win 16 playoff games against the cream of the crop all after qualifying for that tournament.

The 1995 Houston Rockets, who featured some serious ballers, including Hakeem Olajuwon, Clyde Drexler, Vernon Maxwell, Sam Cassell, Kenny Smith and Robert Horry, amongst others, are the lowest seed to ever win an NBA Championship, doing so as the Western Conference's sixth seed. They won 47 games during the regular season and went on to knock off four 50-win clubs in the playoffs. Those teams were the Jazz, Suns, Spurs and Magic, who got broomsticks in the Finals. Some context – the Jazz went on to the Finals in 1997 and 1998, the Spurs in 1999 and beyond, and the Suns in 1993.[108]

Is a little luck involved? Do matchups matter; maybe somebody else knocked off a team that the champs would have had a tougher time matching up with? Absolutely, but the point is that you don't become NBA Champions by accident and any basketball pundit would agree. We are talking about long series; this is not an *any given Sunday, puncher's chance* sport. The better team generally prevails.

Not to say having that one generational talent, that franchise player doesn't greatly sway your odds at becoming champion, but there is always a *Robin* or a gang to go along with *Scooby-Doo*. Teammates and coaches are crucial in any championship run.

So, who had the better teammates and how can we figure it out? For starters, let's look at the teammates in the years that both LeBron and Mike's teams went to the Finals. Who were the teammates? After an in-depth look, we can draw some comparisons, conclusions and weigh-in with an objective verdict.

"But MJ had Pippen!" If I only had a dollar every time I heard this. Just as much as one player doesn't make a team, neither do two players; see Stockton and Malone. Let's not take away from Scottie; he was seven-time All-NBA, seven-time All-Star, ten-time All-Defense, Steals Champ and All-Star MVP, just to name a few.[109] He was Jordan's sidekick and undoubtedly a top-10 second option of all-time. He was the only All-Star Mike ever played alongside (while others were All-Stars, none were ever in the same season as Mike). He was such an effective compliment to MJ because he could guard with the best of them and didn't require the ball in his hands to get going. We have already documented Mike's struggles before Pippen arrived. Quite frankly, he is the most important teammate to MJ and I don't think many would objectively disagree.

Next, Horace Grant, four-time All-Defense, one-time All-Star.[110] A big brute who could bang with the best of them. He was the third member of the Bulls' Big Three in their first three-peat. The others that rounded out the earlier title teams were excellent role players and contributors – John Paxson, Bill Cartwright, B.J. Armstrong, Craig Hodges and Will Perdue.

So, were these teams that great? The obvious answer is yes because they won three consecutive titles; but, on paper, these teams were not star-studded outside of the top two or three guys. The difference was that they played a system, mastered it, did the little things well and hounded the ball on the defensive end.

Following the baseball hiatus, enter a new supporting cast. Grant was upgraded for Rodman, Cartwright swapped for Longley, Armstrong and Paxson for Ron Harper and Steve Kerr and welcome the foreigner, Kukoc. These teams were far superior to the earlier championship teams on paper and the 1996-97 team is still widely regarded as the best or second-best of all-time.

Again, the front office put the right pieces around Jordan and if not for contract disputes with Pippen, who knows if this team goes for four or five-in-a-row? We all know what Rodman added outside of the hair dye. Kukoc became a versatile scorer off the bench when MJ or Pippen needed to be spelled. Kerr was an absolute knockdown spray gun from three. Harper played lockup defense and Longley was in there to bang, board and make sure nothing came easy if you got to the last line of defense.

Not much else to say other than these teams were legit. They played within a system, defended better than anyone else and took down some giants in the playoffs to win six titles. Were they the most skilled teams, did they have the flashiest players, did they have four All-Stars and seven Hall-of-Famers? No, they stuck to the blueprint and donned the jewelry and hardware.

Okay, now for the King. Much different. While Jordan only had one teammate appear alongside him in the All-Star Game, LeBron has had five different teammates appear alongside him and four times had two teammates in the same game.[111] Also, LeBron's teammates during his title runs changed drastically from year-to-year and even between years. You could say the blueprints were ever-changing.

Let's look at his first Finals appearance with the Cavs in

2007. Many contend that this team should not have been taken anywhere near a Finals run and LeBron willed them to win. Couldn't agree more, but let's not call his teammates slouches. Larry Hughes, Drew Gooden, Zydrunas Ilgauskas, Sascha Pavlovic, Daniel Gibson, Anderson Varejao, Donyell Marshall, Damon Jones and Eric Snow. Sure, no clear number two guy, but from a team perspective, they had role players, defensive and three-point specialists, pick-and-roll and pick-and-pop options. Most of these guys were either two years from their prime or slightly over-the-hill. Larry Hughes was really the only player performing within his prime outside of LeBron. So far advantage-Jordan, by a long shot.

Now, here's where things get interesting. South Beach. Big Three. In their first campaign, Miami came up just short of a title, despite having LBJ, D Wade, Bosh, Mike Bibby, Udonis Haslem, Mario Chalmers, Mike Miller and Joel Anthony.

That was a championship-caliber team on paper, no arguments to be made otherwise. From a skill and talent perspective, it also rivals the Bulls teams of the late-1990s. You have three all-stars and at the time, arguably the best two players on the planet LBJ and Wade, similar to what some have said about Jordan and Pippen. Bosh and Rodman were pretty similar in they were stars who played a role, albeit far different roles, but had to sacrifice for the greater good. As far as bench and role players go, the Heat didn't have a Kukoc, but certainly had strength in numbers over those Chicago benches.

Because they didn't win in year one, they re-tooled and upgraded the supporting cast. Bring in Ray Allen, Rashard

Lewis, Chris "Birdman" Andersen and Shane Battier. Battier and Allen are what put the Heat over the edge; both were highly effective from three, either off the screen or spotting up. Battier served as chief irritant and perimeter defender so that James could conserve energy for the stretch runs. Birdman brought the excitement and interior presence and the rest is history.

This squad went back-to-back and nearly went for a three-peat, but age caught up with the role players and LeBron peaced back for Cleveland. These champion Heat teams were head and shoulders above any team Jordan was a part of from a skill and talent perspective. Based on the breakdown, it would be extremely difficult to impartially oppose. If you do, I challenge you to look at who they lost to; it wasn't a team, but rather *father time*. And no, that was not a reference to Greg Popovich...or was it?

A lot of the same can be said for the 1980s Bulls. Over the hill stars like the Iceman, George Gervin, lack of creators outside of MJ, dynasties in Boston and later, Detroit, and a system that was basically summed up as, "Get the ball to Mike" were the ingredients in a recipe for coming up just short of the promised land, the holy grail, a championship.

So, back to Cleveland and he made sure there were no remnants of the 2007 team. *Robin* now came in the form of Kyrie Irving, with Kevin Love to follow. Solid nucleus to say the least. One issue for LBJ here was the injury bug, the other was the unfortunate timing and formation of the biggest hype beast, bandwagon super team of all-time, the Golden State Warriors.

Unrelated, but anybody that knew me and talked basketball with me during this time knows that I rooted for the David Lee and Steph Curry Warriors and said they would be a problem, certainly didn't foresee what came.

2015 was a lot like 2007 after Love and Kyrie went down. Matthew Dellevadova, Iman Shumpert, Tristan Thompson and J.R. Smith can only get you so far. So, back to the drawing board. Lots of pieces were substituted in and out over the next three years: Mozgov, Korver, Channing Frye, George Hill, Jeff Green, Richard Jefferson, Jordan Clarkson, Larry Nance, Derrick Rose, old friends, Dwayne Wade, James Jones and Mike Miller. Again, great teammates and a lot of tenured veterans, but not the right fit and not enough continuity of lineups to win championships.

To sum it up, these teams were loaded with pedigree, talent and acumen. I'd be happy to stack them up against any of Jordan's teams to show that, but you get the idea by this point – LeBron didn't carry shitty teammates, the cards just didn't fall in his favor. Injuries plagued his teams that could have won. The Warriors had a better band of players that fit into a system and despite having the better teams when in Miami, the fit just wasn't right and they were outplayed and out-executed.

So, what are our takeaways? Jordan clearly had the better *teams*, but not the better *teammates*. I won't make an outlandish statement like, "This clearly makes Jordan a better leader," because it wouldn't be true. MJ took less of a role in management and let the guys who get paid for that handle that part (good thing; look at his tenure with Washington and the Bobcats/Hornets). The Bulls stuck to the blueprint; MJ maintained teams in dynasties, with not much alteration at all, while LeBron's requests for certain players and trade deadline theatrics have been well-documented. This isn't really a jab at LeBron as much as it's a preference of the stars in the league today – loyalty is not valued like it once was.

My other big takeaway will probably be very controversial: like Mike in the 1980s, LeBron played the wrong position most of his career and wasn't supplemented appropriately, except by basketball's most underrated mind and architect, Pat Riley.

Did he really just say that? Yes, I recognize LeBron is one of the best passers this game has ever seen. However, did you see how he played as a slasher in Miami? Did you see how he played in the open floor? Could not be stopped! Think about if Cleveland spent less money on wings in J.R. Smith and Shumpert and bigs like Thompson and Mozgov. All four of these guys were heavily overpaid. And that's not to mention Kevin Love. Unlike Bosh, he couldn't play the interior defense in small ball, so he, too, was a poor fit. Look at all that free cap space and think about plugging much cheaper options into the Cleveland system like Trevor Ariza, P.J. Tucker and Boris Diaw. Maybe add a spot-up guard as well, someone like Patty Mills or Goran Dragic. Think about trading Kyrie for Jimmy Butler.

While all of those players were available in 2014 and 2015, were any or all selecting Cleveland as his destination? Probably not. But you never know when you dangle the, "you can play with the King" card. Hindsight is 2020. What I am getting at is great teammates and players do not matter for as much credit as they get in this argument. A better fit and system make all the difference.

VI

Numbers

17

Tally 'Em Up

B efore we dream of comparing these two and saying one is better than the other, let's collectively take a moment, drop to one knee, bow our heads and bask in their greatness. Okay, LeBron fans only *one* knee.

I am not even going to talk about totals because they're irrelevant. Vince Carter and Jason Kidd are in the top 10 in three-pointers made. No disrespect to the legends, but they literally called him "Ason" Kidd because he had no jumper. Longevity is important and we will get to it shortly, but when we're talking about numbers, we have to compare apples to apples and look a bit beyond the face.

I am one of those basketball purists who wonders if you can truly even make a comparison between stats from different eras because of the variables. Let's revisit the points per game argument that we dove into earlier. You don't see Finals games end in sub-triple-digit scores in today's game, whereas, in the 1990s you would have been hard-pressed to find a game with one team in triple-digits. There's that. There's the emphasis of the three-ball, the officiating, average distance of shots, defensive schematics, positionless style, etc. And this doesn't just impact points, but rebounds, assists and steals as well.

Think about how guards in today's game average so many rebounds; it's science. Longer shots, lower field goal percentage, more and longer rebound opportunity and emphasis on preventing transition makes for the perfect recipe for uncontested rebounds from guards waiting at the elbow extended to start the fast break.

Albeit, he is tall for a point guard. Steph Curry has averaged roughly 4.5 rebounds per game for his career.[112] Throw Steph into the 1990s and he might not average one. Again, nothing against him, but he's not getting the opportunity; the game was played in the mid-range and his team and coaches wouldn't have asked him to do that.

On the flip side, you rarely see players crack eight assists in today's game because of the positionless style. Would Stockton have racked up as many assists if he played alongside a Jokic rather than Malone in today's game? Who knows?

It's not to say those guys couldn't develop the skills needed for the other eras; however, it is not a fair comparison. So, I really don't place much emphasis on totals or per game stats when comparing players from different eras. We can take a brief look at numbers, but I am more concerned with *impact* in this debate. Anyone that says, "LeBron has *x* number more points than Jordan, LeBron has *x* number more Finals points, rebounds and assists than everybody, LeBron has more triple-doubles" or "Jordan averaged 37 per, what's the most LeBron averaged?" are giving half-assed arguments.

LeBron averages 27 points, seven rebounds and seven assists with 1.5 steals and one block on 50/34/73, while Jordan averaged 30, six and five with 2.3 and one on 50/33/84.[113][114] I am not going to split hairs, but I will give a scientific spin. After 1,000+ games, they're pretty damn close.

Jordan's scoring is more impressive just because of the lower utilization of the three-ball, fewer possessions per game and emphasis on defense throughout the majority of his career. If I was making some type of difficulty coefficient, I would say Jordan's average of thirty would be closer to 36-37 if he started his career at the same time as LeBron.

LeBron is the superior assist man because passing is more of a team job in today's game. While Jordan was an able passer and we touched on the fact that he got assists when he had to in his first Finals, his average of five would be more like three or four in today's era. Whereas, if LeBron was a point guard in Jordan's era, his seven would be closer to ten or 11.

Rebounds would be pretty dead even however you break it down. If LeBron was a traditional point guard in the earlier era, his boards would likely remain about the same just due to his size. Jordan would probably tick up a couple due to the ball finding him, per my Curry argument from earlier.

Steals and blocks would be roughly the same in either era as both players have amazing defensive instincts. Not sure how many chase downs LeBron would be getting in a slower-paced game or how many Jordan would be getting in a catch-and-shoot league.

Even slash lines, who can really tell? Would LeBron's free throw percentage be even lower in an era where he would be physically beaten up and down the court for forty-eight minutes, his fourth-quarter shooting dips have been documented throughout his career. Does MJ spend more time on the line in a softer era of officiating and handsy defense? Does Mike focus on three-point shooting more and extend his range to shoot more volume from three? All hypotheticals and I really prefer not to touch them for the purity of this discussion.

Let's move onto three stats that are more scientific by nature: PER, WS and VORP.

PER is a formula, essentially standardizing per-minute production, with the league average at about 15. The statistic was developed by *ESPN*'s John Hollinger. In his words, "The PER sums up all a player's positive accomplishments, subtracts the negative accomplishments, and returns a per-minute rating of a player's performance."[115]

Can you guess the top-2 best marks in PER, all-time? I am sure you can. MJ first at 27.91 and LeBron second at 27.49.[116] I told you, splitting hairs.… .

Next is win shares, a player statistic that attempts to divvy up credit for team success to the individuals on the team. It is calculated using player, team and league-wide statistics and the sum of player win shares on a given team will be roughly equal to that team's win total for the season. Kareem Abdul-Jabbar's total of 25.4 win shares in 1971-72 is the all-time, single-season record and his 273.4 career win shares are the all-time career record.[117]

By now you know, I don't like *totals*. And for that reason, I present to you…drum roll…win shares per forty-eight minutes. Number one is MJ at 0.2505. David Robinson, Wilt, CP3, Neil Johnston and LeBron at .2338 round out the top six.[118] As you also know, I only care about stats from when the three-point line was introduced, so, sorry Wilt and Neil, but MJ, the Admiral, CP3, LBJ and Kareem round out my top five.

Value over replacement player, or "VORP", is a box score estimate of the points per 100 TEAM possessions that a player contributed above a replacement player, translated to an average team and prorated to an 82-game season.[119] Before we look at who has a better VORP (yes, they are one and two well ahead of the rest of the pack in this category as well), let's recognize the implicit imperfection of the utilization of the three-ball. Naturally, LeBron's assists and points will be skewed due to his era and style of the game. I am not picking favorites, just announcing implicit limitations in the statistic, the same way we talked about points, rebounds, assists, etc. Bron has an amazing 133.67, Jordan a distant second with 116.08. For reference, John Stockton is third with 106.50; nobody else even cracks triple-digits.[120]

Let's recap. I don't like numbers, but the numbers that

matter most are PER, WS/48, and VORP until some basketball professor creates a better metric. MJ is first in two of three metrics, with LBJ not far behind, yet far ahead in another. I think we can take away the numbers as a stalemate with MJ winning the tiebreaker.

18

Age & Longevity

T he WS/48 and numbers behind the numbers discussion bring us to another important pivot: *age and longevity.*

You cannot just dismiss the fact that LBJ will likely go down as number one in points and between second and fifth in assists, on top of all of his playoffs and Finals records. His longevity is unparalleled. He has taken care of himself since day one and he does not look or perform like somebody his age should. That is a testament to his work ethic, drive and passion.

Jordan did it at the highest level, quit in his prime to play baseball, came back and picked up right where left off until he was 34. He retired again at the height of his career after plenty of wear and tear only to come back and do it again at 38 and 39 after three years away from the game. Keep in mind, Jordan also played three years of college ball before going pro and partied like an animal on game nights.

I truly do not know which is more impressive, but it should be noted that most guys struggle to get to the NBA and those who do make it struggle to get a second contract. To do it for over 15 or 17 years deserves a lifetime achievement award. Based on LeBron's trajectory and no signs of stopping soon, you have to give him the edge here.

19

Unfinished Business

The discussion on numbers would not be complete without MJ's run with the Wizards or LeBron's with the Lakers and beyond. Let's take a moment to thank MJ for coming back the second time and for those who don't know why he did, this will be a treat.

Jordan became a minority owner and president of basketball operations for the Washington Wizards. As a front-office executive, MJ's job description was to be responsible for the roster – managing the cap, making draft picks and other suit stuff that you just know killed his competitive nature. He was more of a Billy Walsh than an Ari Gold.[121] As would be expected, he'd make his way down to the locker room or the trainer's tables with his coffee, chatting up the vets, itching to touch the hardwood. Pause.

In September 2001, two weeks after the 9/11 attacks shook DC and the nation, Jordan announced his intention to return, divesting his ownership stake in the team and donating his salary to relief efforts for the attacks.

The team would be coached by Jordan's former coach in Chicago, Doug Collins. Outside of a young Rip Hamilton, the team was comprised of promising young talent, including the number one pick, Kwame Brown, who turned out to be Jordan's worst contribution to the game of basketball, and a few veteran journeymen.

Jordan was legitimately in the MVP conversation until the All-Star break approached. He had the Wizards hovering above .500 after winning just 19 games the year before. Unfortunately, a knee injury that required surgery effectively ended his season. In 60 games, Jordan averaged 23 points, six rebounds, five assists and 1.4 steals per game, playing 35 minutes a night. MJ led the Wizards in scoring and made the Eastern Conference All-Star team. At that point in the season, the late-great Kobe Bryant (man, that still hasn't sunk in), was the only other player in the league averaging 25, five and five.[122]

The Wizards traded Hubert Davis, Bobby Simmons and Hamilton for Jerry Stackhouse before the 2002 season and added swingman Larry Hughes in free agency.

Jordan scored 40 three times, becoming the first 40-year-old ever to score that many in a game. He played in all 82 games, averaging 20 and six, but the Wizards failed to make the playoffs again, and Mike called it quits for good.[123] Wasn't as good an ending as *The Shot*, but we were all happy to see that Mike still had it.

Can LeBron do something similar with the Lakers? Can he get to the coveted six rings? Dare I ask, can he get seven? Put the right team around him and he just might. Again, hypotheticals…time shall tell.

VII

THE MOMENT WE HAVE ALL BEEN WAITING FOR

20

What Do We Value?

G.O.A.T. talk. What did we decide crowns the *greatest of all-time*? Winning. Elevation in crunch time. Dynasty. Impact. Competition. Consistency. Teammates. Defining Moments. Legacy. Let's not forget – some of it is circumstantial as well – did you change a franchise; did you open up the sport to new audiences?

Did we miss anything? Doubtful, but if I am not actually perfect, as my mother tells me, I am sure these guys are neck-and-neck, photo finish in that category too. Only one thing left to do… .

21

Crown the G.O.A.T.

After all of that, who is the G.O.A.T.? Obviously, it's the *Two. Three.* Do I still have to spell it out? Give that man his cigar and his crown. Of course it is and, if you still cannot say Air Jordan, you're thinking like a fan and not a rational human being, which is fine; I appreciate the diehard fandom. Fine, I will spell it out one final time.

Who was the better winner of the two? Jordan never played in one NBA Finals Game 7, while LeBron has already lost on the biggest stage six times, not to mention a few times where he was bounced from the playoffs earlier than he should have. Again, Jordan was not perfect as 6-0 suggests; the Bucks, Celtics, Pistons and upstart Magic bounced him in the Eastern Conference playoffs. However, he always elevated his play in the Finals and, for that reason, he was the better winner. Seven playoff series losses or six losses in the Finals alone. Bonus stat: from November 1990 to Michael's second retirement after the 1998 Finals, the Bulls never lost more than two-in-a-row when MJ played! Who are you going with?

Clutch factor and defining moments. We have documented LeBron's shortcomings in not quite being able to hoist the trophy. Did he carry some of his teams to a point where they should not have been? Absolutely. But as the saying goes, "You are only as good as your last performance," and unfortunately for him, he walked off the court without celebrating quite a bit; look no further than the 2011 Finals. Don't get me wrong, when his teams did win it was mainly because of his clutch, like in Cleveland's taking down of the goliath 73-9 Warriors thanks to his two-way dominance. But that begs the question, "If the clutch gene was in the *on position* all of the time, would he have more titles?" Jordan, on the other hand, did close out series; just ask Craig Ehlo and Bryon Russell.

Still not a believer? Okay, bonus stat time: in potential game-tying and/or go-ahead field goal attempts in the postseason, no player has better numbers than MJ, who was nine for 18 in such attempts. Nobody has made more attempts than LeBron (opportunity was greater due to games played and usage) who shot 10 for 27 or 37%. That is not a great mark for anyone, let alone for a player that has shot 50% from the field for his career. How about LeBron has shot below 40% for two different NBA Finals, while MJ never put up such poor shooting numbers on the biggest stage.

Again, all the focus is on him in those games and possessions and he's obviously that dude for getting 27 attempts, but he doesn't measure up to the *G.O.A.T.*

Competition and teammates are hard to measure cross-era, as we have discussed. LeBron's teams are credited as being historically bad, but let's give another bonus stat takeaway that puts that argument in perspective. The top two lowest supporting cast scoring averages on a winning Finals team are Jordan's 1998 and 1997 Bulls, respectively averaging 54.5 and 55.5 points per game. I don't see LeBron's 2016 Cavs or Heat teams on that list.

In the 2014 Finals, Wade and Bosh combined for 29.2 points per game and many let LeBron off the hook for losing that series to the 62-20 Spurs. What is often forgotten: Pippen and Kukoc averaged only 28.0 points per game in the 1997 Finals against the 64-18 Jazz. Again, important to note that total scoring averages don't translate one-for-one, but Jordan did it while carrying most of the scoring burden. So, when it comes to carrying, 34 and 35-year old Michael takes the cake.

Consistency. Jordan was Jordan. He was consistent in his stats and winning. LeBron also consistently is the best all-around basketball player on the planet. I can objectively give the edge to LeBron based solely on the fact that he has done it longer than Jordan did and never took time away from the game.

I have nothing left to say, but I will ask, "Did I confirm your belief, or did I change your mind?"

What will it take to de-crown the *G.O.A.T.*? Will six rings push a tie for LeBron? Will upping his PER and WS/48 do it? Will him three-peating with the Lakers make him the *G.O.A.T.*? What about for anyone else? Who has the trajectory?

I think it's fair to say that if LeBron gets seven, he takes the crown. However, at what expense? If he is 7-10 in Finals appearances, how can you really say that he is the *G.O.A.T.* knowing what we now know about his losses?

Since we have been so good about not introducing or giving weight to hypotheticals and opinions, how about we reward ourselves with a few before we go?

What if MJ never played baseball and won in 1994 and 1995? To the non-believers, would LeBron still be better if MJ was 8-0 in the Finals? What if the team stuck together for 1998 and they won again?

How about a wild one...what if His Airness got drafted by Houston or Portland, do you think we'd still be having this conversation?

What if he doesn't need that knee surgery in his first season with the Wizards and wins a title with them, or at least makes a run to the ECF?

Okay, now Lebron. What if LeBron wins before leaving Cleveland? What if the Big Three re-tooled after the loss to the Spurs and rode it out for a few more years?

Oh man, don't you wish we could play out all of the could haves and should haves? Or, you can just sit there and thank the basketball gods for giving us the gifts they have.

22

Final Thoughts

I am glad we are all in agreement on MJ being number one, sarcasm – I know you're all trying to get refunds right now. But seriously, if I don't have LeBron at number one, where do I have him? Lucky for you, you can have a little bonus. Here's my Top-25 as of the end of the 2018-2019 season:

Overall Rank	Player	Rings	Finals MVP
1	Michael Jordan	6	6
2	Magic Johnson	5	3
3	Shaquille O'Neal	4	3
4	Kobe Bryant	5	2
5	Larry Bird	3	2
6	Kareem Abdul-Jabbar	6	2
7	LeBron James	3*	3
8	Tim Duncan	5	3
9	Hakeem Olajuwon	2	2
10	Kevin Durant	2*	2
11	Steph Curry	3*	-
12	Dwyane Wade	3	1
13	Dirk Nowitzki	2	1
14	Scottie Pippen	6	-
15	Isiah Thomas	2	1
16	Charles Barkley	0	-
17	David Robinson	2	-
18	Karl Malone	0	-
19	Kevin Garnett	1	-
20	Allen Iverson	0	-
21	Kawhi Leonard	2*	1
22	Jason Kidd	1	-
23	Steve Nash	0	-
24	John Stockton	0	-
25	Dennis Rodman	5	-

Obviously, things will likely have happened between then and publication, so relax and take a look from that lens. You probably still won't like it, but it is what it is! I could easily see LeBron getting to second-best best by merely winning one more legitimate Finals MVP. As for now, on my list, he barely edges out Tim Duncan for seventh. Let me know what you think and maybe I can piss you off in another book on that topic.

Endnotes

[1]De Niro, R. (1993). A Bronx Tale. Savoy Pictures.

[2]*This is SportsCenter* [SportsCenter]. Bristol, CT: ESPN

[3]Russ Smith sets D-League single-game scoring record https://www.espn.com/nba/story/_/id/15055640/russ-smith-sets-d-league-scoring-record-65-points

[4]Russ Smith says 'it's BS' he's not in NBA after averaging 60-plus points in China

Kalbrosky; https://hoopshype.com/2017/09/08/russ-smith-says-its-bs-hes-not-in-nba-after-averaging-60-plus-points-per-game-in-china-return-comeback/

[5]Edwards, Herm (2002, October 30). New York Jets Post-Game Interview. [Open Press Conference].

[6]Johnson, Logic (2012, April 10). LeBron James and the 10 Greatest Players Drafted out of High School. *Bleacherreport.com*

[7]Drake. (2010). Bollywood Flow (Tim Westwood Freestyle).

[8]Dreamville (2019). Down Bad. [Recorded by J. Cole (Dreamville)]. On *Revenge of the Dreamers III*. Raleigh, NC: Dreamville Records.

[9]https://basketball.fandom.com/wiki/LeBron_James -:~:text=James finished his high school,892 rebounds and 523 assists.

[10]Trivic, Filip. (2019, August 10). *JAMES WORTHY: "I was better than Jordan"*. BaketballNetwork.net. https://www.basketballnetwork.net/i-was-better-than-michael-jordan/

[11]Reevy, Matt. (2015, September 5). *The 5 Youngest NBA Finals MVPs Ever.* Sportscasting.com. https://www.sportscasting.com/5-youngest-nba-finals-mvps-now-featuring-kawhi-leonard-2/

[12] *"Finals Most Valuable Player".* NBA/Turner Sports Interactive, Inc. Retrieved July 14, 2008. https://www.nba.com/history/awards/finals-mvp

[13]Chicago Bulls All-Star Game Selections https://www.basketball-reference.com/teams/CHI/all_star.html

[14]Chicago Bulls Franchise Index https://www.basketball-reference.com/teams/CHI/

[15]List of career achievements by Michael Jordan https://en.wikipedia.org/wiki/List_of_career_achievements_by_Michael_Jordan

[16]Verdi, Bob. (1985, February 7). *BIRD IS SOLD ON JORDAN, NBA'S FUTURE. Chicago Tribune.* https://www.chicagotribune.com/news/ct-xpm-1985-02-07-8501080020-story.html

[17]1984-85 Milwaukee Bucks Roster and Stats https://www.basketball-reference.com/teams/MIL/1985.html

[18]1985 NBA Eastern Conference First Round - Bulls vs. Bucks https://www.basketball-reference.com/playoffs/1985-nba-eastern-conference-first-round-bulls-vs-bucks.html

[19]1986 NBA Eastern Conference First Round - Bulls vs. Celtics
https://www.basketball-reference.com/playoffs/1986-nba-eastern-conference-first-round-bulls-vs-celtics.html

[20]Michael Jordan Stats https://www.basketball-reference.com/players/j/jordami01.html

[21]Montalbo, Ike. (2010, November 9). *NBA Power Rankings: Michael Jordan's Top 10 Scoring Seasons.* BleacherReport.com.

[22]Carroll, Charlotte. (2019, February 16). *Check Out Every NBA Slam Dunk Contest Winner In History*. *Sports Illustrated*. https://www.si.com/nba/2019/02/16/nba-slam-dunk-contest-past-winners-complete-list

[23]Montalbo, Ike. (2010, November 9). *NBA Power Rankings: Michael Jordan's Top 10 Scoring Seasons*. BleacherReport.com.

[24]Montalbo, Ike. (2010, November 9). *NBA Power Rankings: Michael Jordan's Top 10 Scoring Seasons*. BleacherReport.com.

[25]1988 NBA Eastern Conference First Round - Cavaliers vs. Bulls
https://www.basketball-reference.com/playoffs/1988-nba-eastern-conference-first-round-cavaliers-vs-bulls.html

[26]1988 NBA Eastern Conference Semifinals - Bulls vs. Pistons
https://www.basketball-reference.com/playoffs/1988-nba-eastern-conference-semifinals-bulls-vs-pistons.html

[27]Montalbo, Ike. (2010, November 9). *NBA Power Rankings: Michael Jordan's Top 10 Scoring Seasons*. BleacherReport.com.

[28]Michael Jordan 1987-88 Game Loghttps://www.basketball-reference.com/players/j/jordami01/gamelog/1988/

[29]Michael Jordan 1987-88 Game Loghttps://www.basketball-reference.com/players/j/jordami01/gamelog/1988/

[30]Montalbo, Ike. (2010, November 9). *NBA Power Rankings: Michael Jordan's Top 10 Scoring Seasons*. BleacherReport.com.

[31]1989 NBA Eastern Conference Finals - Bulls vs. Pistons
https://www.basketball-reference.com/playoffs/1989-nba-eastern-conference-finals-bulls-vs-pistons.html

[32]Cleveland Cavaliers at Sacramento Kings Box Score, October 29, 2003 https://www.basketball-reference.com/

boxscores/200310290SAC.html

[33]2002-03 Cleveland Cavaliers Roster and Stats https:// www.basketball-reference.com/teams/CLE/2003.html

[34]LeBron James Stats https://www.basketball-reference. com/players/j/jamesle01.html

[35]LeBron James vs. Michael Jordan: Comparing Their First 9 Seasons in the NBA. M., Daniel https://bleacherreport. com/articles/1235634-lebron-james-vs-michael-jordan-comparing-their-first-9-seasons-in-the-nba

[36]2004-05 Cleveland Cavaliers Roster and Stats https:// www.basketball-reference.com/teams/CLE/2005.html

[37]2005-06 Cleveland Cavaliers Roster and Stats https:// www.basketball-reference.com/teams/CLE/2006.html

[38]LeBron James vs. Michael Jordan: Comparing Their First 9 Seasons in the NBA. M., Daniel https://bleacherreport. com/articles/1235634-lebron-james-vs-michael-jordan-comparing-their-first-9-seasons-in-the-nba

[39]2006 NBA Eastern Conference First Round - Wizards vs. Cavaliers https://www.basketball-reference.com/ playoffs/2006-nba-eastern-conference-first-round-wizards-vs-cavaliers.html

[40]2006 NBA Eastern Conference Semifinals - Cavaliers vs. Pistons https://www.basketball-reference.com/playoffs/2006-nba-eastern-conference-semifinals-cavaliers-vs-pistons.html

[41] LeBron James vs. Michael Jordan: Comparing Their First 9 Seasons in the NBA. M., Daniel https://bleacherreport. com/articles/1235634-lebron-james-vs-michael-jordan-comparing-their-first-9-seasons-in-the-nba

[42]LeBron James 2006-07 Game Log https://www.basketball-reference.com/players/j/jamesle01/gamelog/2007/

[43]2007 NBA Finals - Cavaliers vs. Spurs https://www.

basketball-reference.com/playoffs/2007-nba-finals-cavaliers-vs-spurs.html

[44] LeBron James vs. Michael Jordan: Comparing Their First 9 Seasons in the NBA. M., Daniel https://bleacherreport.com/articles/1235634-lebron-james-vs-michael-jordan-comparing-their-first-9-seasons-in-the-nba

[45] 2008 NBA Eastern Conference Semifinals - Cavaliers vs. Celtics https://www.basketball-reference.com/playoffs/2008-nba-eastern-conference-semifinals-cavaliers-vs-celtics.html

[46] LeBron James vs. Michael Jordan: Comparing Their First 9 Seasons in the NBA. M., Daniel https://bleacherreport.com/articles/1235634-lebron-james-vs-michael-jordan-comparing-their-first-9-seasons-in-the-nba

[47] LeBron James 2008-09 Game Log https://www.basketball-reference.com/players/j/jamesle01/gamelog/2009/

[48] 2009 NBA Eastern Conference Finals - Magic vs. Cavaliers https://www.basketball-reference.com/playoffs/2009-nba-eastern-conference-finals-magic-vs-cavaliers.html

[49] LeBron James vs. Michael Jordan: Comparing Their First 9 Seasons in the NBA. M., Daniel https://bleacherreport.com/articles/1235634-lebron-james-vs-michael-jordan-comparing-their-first-9-seasons-in-the-nba

[50] 2010 NBA Eastern Conference Semifinals - Celtics vs. Cavaliers https://www.basketball-reference.com/playoffs/2010-nba-eastern-conference-semifinals-celtics-vs-cavaliers.html

[51] "The Decision". *ESPN*. Greenwich, CT. July 8, 2010. *Television*.

[52] Nolan, Christopher, director. *The Dark Knight*. Warner Bros. Pictures, 2008.

[53] James, LeBron. "On Stage Interview with Wade, Bosh and

James". Interview by Eric Reid. 2010, July 9.

[54]LeBron James 2010-11 Game Log https://www.basketball-reference.com/players/j/jamesle01/gamelog/2011/

[55]2010-11 Miami Heat Roster and Stats https://www.basketball-reference.com/teams/MIA/2011.html

[56]LeBron James Stats https://www.basketball-reference.com/players/j/jamesle01.html

[57]2010-11 NBA Awards Voting https://www.basketball-reference.com/awards/awards_2011.html

[58]Land Of Basketball.com https://www.landofbasketball.com/nba_players/j/lebron_james.htm

[59]LeBron James 2010-11 Game Log https://www.basketball-reference.com/players/j/jamesle01/gamelog/2011/

[60]*30 for 30* https://www.imdb.com/title/tt1408430/

[61]2011 NBA Finals - Mavericks vs. Heat https://www.basketball-reference.com/playoffs/2011-nba-finals-mavericks-vs-heat.html

[62]Legends profile: Michael Jordan Staff & NBA.com https://www.nba.com/history/legends/profiles/michael-jordan

[63]1991 NBA Finals - Lakers vs. Bulls https://www.basketball-reference.com/playoffs/1991-nba-finals-lakers-vs-bulls.html

[64]Top Moments: Michael Jordan blazes away from long range to burn Blazers Staff & NBA.com https://www.nba.com/history/top-moments/1992-jordan-shrug-blazers-finals

[65]Michael Jordan 1992-93 Game Log https://www.basketball-reference.com/players/j/jordami01/gamelog/1993/

[66]1993 NBA Finals - Bulls vs. Suns https://www.basketball-reference.com/playoffs/1993-nba-finals-bulls-vs-suns.html

[67]Chicago Bulls at New York Knicks Box Score, March

28, 1995 https://www.basketball-reference.com/boxscores/199503280NYK.html

[68] 1995-96 Chicago Bulls Roster and Stats https://www.basketball-reference.com/teams/CHI/1996.html

[69] Legends profile: Michael Jordan Staff & NBA.com https://www.nba.com/history/legends/profiles/michael-jordan

[70] 1996 NBA Playoffs Summary https://www.basketball-reference.com/playoffs/NBA_1996.html

[71] 1996-97 NBA Season Summary https://www.basketball-reference.com/leagues/NBA_1997.html

[72] Caffey, T. (Writer). (2020, April 19). *The Last Dance* [Television series]. ESPN.

[73] Legends profile: Michael Jordan Staff & NBA.com https://www.nba.com/history/legends/profiles/michael-jordan

[74] 1998 NBA Eastern Conference Finals - Pacers vs. Bulls https://www.basketball-reference.com/playoffs/1998-nba-eastern-conference-finals-pacers-vs-bulls.html

[75] Land Of Basketball.com https://www.landofbasketball.com/nba_players/j/lebron_james.htm

[76] 2011-12 Miami Heat Roster and Stats https://www.basketball-reference.com/teams/MIA/2012.html

[77] Miami Heat at Boston Celtics Box Score, June 7, 2012 https://www.basketball-reference.com/boxscores/201206070BOS.html

[78] Boston Celtics at Miami Heat Box Score, June 9, 2012 https://www.basketball-reference.com/boxscores/201206090MIA.html

[79] Land Of Basketball.com https://www.landofbasketball.com/nba_players/j/lebron_james.htm

[80] San Antonio Spurs at Miami Heat Box Score, June 18, 2013 https://www.basketball-reference.com/boxscores/

201306180MIA.html

[81]San Antonio Spurs at Miami Heat Box Score, June 20, 2013 https://www.basketball-reference.com/boxscores/201306200MIA.html

[82]LeBron James 2013-14 Game Log https://www.basketball-reference.com/players/j/jamesle01/gamelog/2014/

[83]2014 NBA Finals - Heat vs. Spurs https://www.basketball-reference.com/playoffs/2014-nba-finals-heat-vs-spurs.html

[84]2014 NBA Finals - Heat vs. Spurs https://www.basketball-reference.com/playoffs/2014-nba-finals-heat-vs-spurs.html

[85]2014 NBA Finals - Heat vs. Spurs https://www.basketball-reference.com/playoffs/2014-nba-finals-heat-vs-spurs.html

[86]Land Of Basketball.com https://www.landofbasketball.com/nba_players/j/lebron_james.htm

[87]2014-15 Cleveland Cavaliers Roster and Stats https://www.basketball-reference.com/teams/CLE/2015.html

[88]2015 NBA Finals - Cavaliers vs. Warriors https://www.basketball-reference.com/playoffs/2015-nba-finals-cavaliers-vs-warriors.html

[89]2015-16 Cleveland Cavaliers Roster and Stats https://www.basketball-reference.com/teams/CLE/2016.html

[90]2015-16 Golden State Warriors Roster and Stats https://www.basketball-reference.com/teams/GSW/2016.html

[91]Larry Bird Stats https://www.basketball-reference.com/players/b/birdla01.html

[92]Brook Lopez Stats https://www.basketball-reference.com/players/l/lopezbr01.html

[93]James Harden Stats https://www.basketball-reference.com/players/h/hardeja01.html

[94]1984-85 Milwaukee Bucks Roster and Stats https://www.basketball-reference.com/teams/MIL/1985.html

[95]Terry Cummings Stats https://www.basketball-reference.com/players/c/cummite01.html

[96]Land Of Basketball.com https://www.landofbasketball.com/nba_players/m/sidney_moncrief.htm

[97]1985-86 Boston Celtics Roster and Stats https://www.basketball-reference.com/teams/BOS/1986.html

[98]1986-87 Boston Celtics Roster and Stats https://www.basketball-reference.com/teams/BOS/1987.html

[99]1987-88 Detroit Pistons Roster and Stats https://www.basketball-reference.com/teams/DET/1988.html

[100]1988-89 Detroit Pistons Roster and Stats https://www.basketball-reference.com/teams/DET/1989.html

[101]1989-90 Detroit Pistons Roster and Stats https://www.basketball-reference.com/teams/DET/1990.html

[102]Michael Jordan 1994-95 Game Log https://www.basketball-reference.com/players/j/jordami01/gamelog/1995/

[103]1994-95 Orlando Magic Roster and Stats https://www.basketball-reference.com/teams/ORL/1995.html

[104]New York Knicks at Chicago Bulls Box Score, May 19, 1989 https://www.basketball-reference.com/boxscores/198905190CHI.html

[105]1990 NBA Eastern Conference Semifinals - 76ers vs. Bulls https://www.basketball-reference.com/playoffs/1990-nba-eastern-conference-semifinals-76ers-vs-bulls.html

[106]Former Suns star Tom Chambers heads 'famous' list https://www.azcentral.com/story/sports/heat-index/2014/08/18/phoenix-suns-hall-fame-tom-chambers-nba/14251261/

[107]Stevenson, D. (2017, August 21). [Interview by N. Angstadt]. *Locked on Mavericks*.

[108]1994-95 Houston Rockets Roster and Stats https://www.

basketball-reference.com/teams/HOU/1995.html

[109]Land Of Basketball.com https://www.landofbasketball. com/nba_players/p/scottie_pippen.htm

[110]Horace Grant Stats https://www.basketball-reference. com/players/g/grantho01.html

[111]NBA & ABA All-Star Game Stats and History https:// www.basketball-reference.com/allstar/

[112]Stephen Curry Stats https://www.basketball-reference. com/players/c/curryst01.html

[113]LeBron James Stats https://www.basketball-reference. com/players/j/jamesle01.html

[114]Michael Jordan Stats https://www.basketball-reference. com/players/j/jordami01.html

[115]Hollinger, J. (2007, April 26). [Editorial]. ESPN.com. Retrieved October 20, 2020, from https://www.espn.com/nba/-columns/story?columnist=hollinger_john&id=2850240

[116]NBA & ABA Career Leaders and Records for Player Efficiency Rating https://www.basketball-reference.com/leaders/ per_career.html

[117]NBA Win Shares https://www.basketball-reference. com/about/ws.html

[118]NBA & ABA Career Leaders and Records for Win Shares Per 48 Minutes https://www.basketball-reference. com/leaders/ws_per_48_career.html

[119]Glossary https://www.basketball-reference.com/about/ glossary.html

[120]NBA & ABA Career Leaders and Records for Value Over Replacement Player https://www.basketball-reference.com/ leaders/vorp_career.html

[121]*Entourage*. Created by Doug Ellin, *HBO*, 18 July 2004.

[122]Smith, E. (2020, June). [Editorial]. *Fansided*. Retrieved Oc-

tober, 2020, from https://wizofawes.com/2020/05/24/washington
wizards-michael-jordan-last-dance/

[123]Smith, E. (2020, June). [Editorial]. *Fansided*. Retrieved October, 2020, from https://wizofawes.com/2020/05/24/washington
wizards-michael-jordan-last-dance/

Made in the USA
Middletown, DE
15 November 2020